THE
COMING
ANARCHY

THE
COMING
ANARCHY

Shattering the Dreams
of the Post Cold War

ROBERT D. KAPLAN

RANDOM HOUSE NEW YORK

All of the essays in this work were originally published in *The Atlantic
Monthly* except as follows:
"Conrad's *Nostromo* and the Third World" was originally published in
The National Interest, and "The Dangers of Peace" has not been previ-
ously published.
"Idealism Won't Stop Mass Murder" was originally published in the
November 14, 1997, issue of *The Wall Street Journal.* Copyright © 1997
by Dow Jones & Company, Inc. All rights reserved. Reprinted with per-
mission of *The Wall Street Journal.*

Library of Congress Cataloging-in-Publication Data

Kaplan, Robert D.
The coming anarchy: shattering the dreams of the post Cold
War/Robert D. Kaplan.
p.   cm.
ISBN 0-375-50354-4 (acid-free paper)
1. World politics—1989–   2. Post-communism.   I. Title.
D860.K353   2000
909.82'9—dc21   99-41034

Random House website address: www.atrandom.com
Printed in the United States of America on acid-free paper
4 6 8 9 7 5 3

Book design by Barbara M. Bachman

To Edit Bornstein,
Avner Goren,
Richard Lobell,
Richard and Varda Nowitz,
and Harry Wall

BEFORE THE NAMES OF JUST AND UNJUST
CAN HAVE PLACE,
THERE MUST BE SOME COERCIVE POWER.

—*Thomas Hobbes,* LEVIATHAN

PREFACE

The years that follow an epochal military and political victory such as the fall of the Berlin Wall are lonely times for realists. The victors naturally assume that their struggle carries deep significance, of a kind that cannot fail to redeem the world. Indeed, the harder and longer the struggle, the greater its meaning in the mind of the winning side, and the greater the benefits it sees for humanity. Victory in World War I saw a burst of such idealism under the banner of "Wilsonianism," a notion that took little account of the real goals of America's European allies and even less account of the realities in the Balkans and the Near East, where democracy and freedom meant heightened ethnic awareness. The same pattern followed the West's victory in the Cold War, which many believed would bring simply freedom and prosperity under the banners of "democracy" and "free markets." But just as after World War I and World War II, our victory has ushered in the next struggle for survival, in which evil wears new masks.

I do not gloat over these facts, for I was a fervent Cold Warrior seeking a better world. As a journalist I covered Eastern Europe when it was unfashionable to do so: in the 1980s, when the media elite was preoccupied with Nicaragua, El Salvador, and Lebanon. I also covered the Soviet occupation of Afghanistan, to which the media gave as little attention as it did to Eastern Europe, even though the Soviets killed ten times more Muslims in Afghanistan than the total number of people killed during the entire Lebanese civil war. And I covered the Horn of Africa long enough to know that the great Ethiopian famine of 1984–1985 was less a matter of drought than of Stalinist terror tactics employed by Ethiopia's Marxist government, like the famine that decimated Soviet Ukraine in the 1930s.

But my reaction in print to the weakening and eventual collapse of the Soviet empire in Eastern Europe was not altogether joyful. My experience in the Balkans throughout the 1980s showed me that the dismantling of Cold War security structures, coupled with the deterioration of southeastern European economies and the history of ethnic conflict in places like Yugoslavia, meant that the end of the Cold War would lead to another redivision of Europe: instead of Western Europe and Eastern Europe there would be Central Europe and the Balkans.

Later, I began to suspect that the optimistic future many predicted for a democratizing sub-Saharan Africa in the wake of the Cold War was no less naïve than the Wilsonianism of a previous era. This is where this book begins. "The Coming Anarchy," whose opening paragraphs describe the West African country of Sierra Leone—where elections in 1996 were followed by the anarchy of bloodthirsty *Lord of the Flies* teenagers in 1999—was researched and written in 1993 and published in February 1994. The overall thesis of a bifurcated world divided between societies like ours, producing goods and services that the rest of the world wants, and those mired in various forms of chaos has held, if not been amplified since then. Indeed, "The Coming Anarchy" has taken on a life of its own and continues to be used as a paradigm for the post–Cold War era, meaning it is a sufficiently worthy target for attack. The concrete reality of the phenomenon it describes is undeniable: for every sixty-five dollars earned in rich countries, one dollar is earned in poor ones, and the gap is widening. That division is not only between "North" and "South," but within countries and regions themselves, including the United States, where an upper-middle techno-class joins the global economy, while a vast realm of the citizenry has seen little rise in their salaries and own no stocks or mutual funds.

"The Coming Anarchy" opens with a dire description of Africa, where at the moment nearly a dozen wars are in progress as the boundaries fixed by colonialist powers unravel, and the criminalization of regimes involved in money laundering and drug smuggling proceeds apace; at the same time, the return of democracy to Nigeria has caused an upsurge in ethnic violence. But Africa is not a bellwether for politics for the rest of the world, as I indicated six years ago when I wrote the article. I still believe, though, that so-called democratic success stories like Nigeria are epiphenomena in a larger pattern of demographic and environmental upheaval.

Even in the Indian subcontinent, where development has been impressive, unrest and breakdown loom: development, as much as poverty, can lead to war. Many of the statistics in my article are now out-of-date, but the worldwide fall in the rate of population increase does not affect my thesis. "The Coming Anarchy" is less concerned with the world's population in the distant future than with steep, *absolute* rises in population in the world's poorest countries in the near future and how that interacts with soil depletion, ethnic-tribal divides, and so on to produce unrest.

"Was Democracy Just a Moment?" was written in November 1996 and published thirteen months later in December 1997, months before the Russian financial crisis made it apparent that democracy had done less to improve the lives of Russia's citizens than autocracy had done for China's. The real message here is not the failure of democracy—but the emergence of quasi-democratic "hybrid" regimes, where parliamentary practices are officially adhered to, while behind the scenes the military and security services play dominant roles. Venezuela seems to be the latest example of this trend.

"Idealism Won't Stop Mass Murder" appeared in November 1997. The ten weeks of NATO bombing against Slobodan Milosevic's regime in Serbia in the spring of 1999 illustrates the ruthlessness required to stop a war criminal in his tracks and, hopefully, to bring him to justice.

The first essays in this book identify the terrors of the post Cold War, while the latter ones seek a historical and philosophical framework with which to approach them. The essays are realistic in the sense that they seek to grapple with how the world actually works, rather than to describe a better world that may never be. They seek to be an unrelenting record of uncomfortable truths, of the kind that many of us implicitly acknowledge but will not publicly accept. The realism exhibited here may appear radical to those in the literary, journalistic, and academic communities, but I can assure the reader that they track well with the analyses of the military and intelligence communities, where accountability is based less on false displays of idealism than on the ability to pinpoint trouble spots a few years down the road.

AFTER "THE COMING ANARCHY" appeared in February 1994 in *The Atlantic Monthly,* I heard murmurs about how editors elsewhere would have wanted to run such an article. I was skeptical, however. I suspected that had they received "The Coming Anarchy" in manuscript form, they would have asked me to reduce its length or split it into several pieces or do something that would have prevented it from eventually being translated into over a dozen languages and reprinted constantly—ever since William Whitworth, editor of *The Atlantic Monthly,* published it with minimal changes. Without Bill Whitworth and Cullen Murphy, *The Atlantic*'s managing editor, who were responsible for originally publishing most of the pieces in this collection, I'm not certain I would still be a full-time writer: I might well have pursued other available means of subsistence. The debt I owe *The Atlantic*, its editors and fact checkers—especially Corby Kummer, Barbara Wallraff, Avril Cornel, Sue Parilla, Martha Spaulding, and Amy Meeker—is immense.

Not all of these pieces appeared in *The Atlantic*. I thank Max Boot of *The Wall Street Journal* editorial page and Owen Harries of *The National Interest* for also providing an outlet for my ideas.

"The Dangers of Peace" is the book's concluding essay. It was completed before the NATO bombing campaign commenced in March 1999, but is published for the first time here.

It was not inevitable that these essays should appear in a book. Two people respected my work sufficiently to make sure that this volume appeared: my literary agent, Carl D. Brandt, and my editor at Random House, Jason Epstein. Joy de Menil at Random House has also been indispensable. I thank them all, truly.

ROBERT D. KAPLAN
August 1999

CONTENTS

THE
COMING
ANARCHY

I.

***

The Coming Anarchy

(February 1994)

The minister's eyes were like egg yolks, an after-effect of some of the many illnesses, malaria especially, endemic in his country. There was also an irrefutable sadness in his eyes. He spoke in a slow and creaking voice, the voice of hope about to expire. Flame trees, coconut palms, and a ballpoint-blue Atlantic composed the background. None of it seemed beautiful, though. "In forty-five years I have never seen things so bad. We did not manage ourselves well after the British departed. But what we have now is something worse—the revenge of the poor, of the social failures, of the people least able to bring up children in a modern society." Then he referred to the recent coup in the West African country Sierra Leone. "The boys who took power in Sierra Leone come from houses like this." The Minister jabbed his finger at a corrugated metal shack teeming with children. "In three months these boys confiscated all the official Mercedes, Volvos, and BMWs and will-fully wrecked them on the road." The Minister mentioned one of the coup's leaders, Solomon Anthony Joseph Musa, who shot the people who had paid for his schooling, "in order to erase the humiliation and mitigate the power his middle-class sponsors held over him."

Tyranny is nothing new in Sierra Leone or in the rest of West Africa. But it is now part and parcel of an increasing law-lessness that is far more significant than any coup, rebel incursion, or episodic experiment in democracy. Crime was what my friend—a top-ranking African official whose life would be threatened were I to identify him more precisely—really wanted to talk about. Crime is what makes West Africa a natural point of departure for my report on what the political character of our planet is likely to be in the twenty-first century.

The cities of West Africa at night are some of the unsafest places in the world. Streets are unlit; the police often lack gasoline for their vehicles; armed burglars, carjackers, and muggers proliferate. "The government in Sierra Leone has no writ after dark," says a foreign resident, shrugging. When I was in the capital, Freetown, last September, eight men armed with AK-47s broke into the house of an American man. They tied him up and stole everything of value. Forget Miami: direct flights between the United States and the Murtala Muhammed Airport, in neighboring Nigeria's largest city, Lagos, have been suspended by order of the U.S. Secretary of Transportation be-cause of ineffective security at the terminal and its environs. A

State Department report cited the airport for "extortion by law-enforcement and immigration officials." This is one of the few times that the U.S. government has embargoed a foreign airport for reasons that are linked purely to crime. In Abidjan, effectively the capital of the Côte d'Ivoire, or Ivory Coast, restaurants have stick- and gun-wielding guards who walk you the fifteen feet or so between your car and the entrance, giving you an eerie taste of what American cities might be like in the future. An Italian ambassador was killed by gunfire when robbers invaded an Abidjan restaurant. The family of the Nigerian ambassador was tied up and robbed at gunpoint in the ambassador's residence. After university students in the Ivory Coast caught bandits who had been plaguing their dorms, they executed them by hanging tires around their necks and setting the tires on fire. In one instance Ivorian policemen stood by and watched the "necklacings," afraid to intervene. Each time I went to the Abidjan bus terminal, groups of young men with restless, scanning eyes surrounded my taxi, putting their hands all over the windows, demanding "tips" for carrying my luggage even though I had only a rucksack. In cities in six West African countries I saw similar young men everywhere—hordes of them. They were like loose molecules in a very unstable social fluid, a fluid that was clearly on the verge of igniting.

"You see," my friend the Minister told me, "in the villages of Africa it is perfectly natural to feed at any table and lodge in any hut. But in the cities this communal existence no longer holds. You must pay for lodging and be invited for food. When young men find out that their relations cannot put them up, they become lost. They join other migrants and slip gradually into the criminal process.

"In the poor quarters of Arab North Africa," he continued, "there is much less crime, because Islam provides a social anchor: of education and indoctrination. Here in West Africa we have a lot of superficial Islam and superficial Christianity. Western religion is undermined by animist beliefs not suitable to a moral society, because they are based on irrational spirit power. Here spirits are used to wreak vengeance by one person against another, or one group against another." Many of the atrocities in the Liberian civil war have been tied to belief in *juju* spirits, and the BBC has reported, in its magazine *Focus on Africa*, that in the civil fighting in adjacent Sierra Leone, rebels were said to have "a young woman with them who would go to the front naked, always walking backwards and looking in a mirror to see where she was going. This made her invisible, so that she could cross to the army's positions and there bury charms . . . to improve the rebels' chances of success."

Finally my friend the Minister mentioned polygamy. Designed for a pastoral way of life, polygamy continues to thrive in sub-Saharan Africa even though it is increasingly uncommon in Arab North Africa. Most youths I met on the road in West Africa told me that they were from "extended" families, with a mother in one place and a father in another. Translated to an urban environment, loose family structures are largely responsible for the world's highest birth rates and the explosion of the HIV virus on the continent. Like the communalism and animism, they provide a weak shield against the corrosive social effects of life in cities. In those cities African culture is being redefined while desertification and deforestation—also tied to overpopulation—drive more and more African peasants out of the countryside.

A PREMONITION OF THE FUTURE

WEST AFRICA IS BECOMING *the* symbol of worldwide demographic, environmental, and societal stress, in which criminal anarchy emerges as the real "strategic" danger. Disease, overpopulation, unprovoked crime, scarcity of resources, refugee migrations, the increasing erosion of nation-states and international borders, and the empowerment of private armies, security firms, and international drug cartels are now most tellingly demonstrated through a West African prism. West Africa provides an appropriate introduction to the issues, often extremely unpleasant to discuss, that will soon confront our civilization. To remap the political earth the way it will be a few decades hence—as I intend to do in this article—I find I must begin with West Africa.

There is no other place on the planet where political maps are so deceptive—where, in fact, they tell such lies—as in West Africa. Start with Sierra Leone. According to the map, it is a nation-state of defined borders, with a government in control of its territory. In truth the Sierra Leonian government, run by a twenty-seven-year-old army captain, Valentine Strasser, controls Freetown by day and by day also controls part of the rural interior. In the government's territory the national army is an unruly rabble threatening drivers and passengers at most checkpoints. In the other part of the country units of two separate armies from the war in Liberia have taken up residence, as has an army of Sierra Leonian rebels. The government force fighting the rebels is full of renegade commanders who have aligned themselves with disaffected village chiefs. A premodern formlessness governs the battlefield, evoking the wars in medieval Europe prior to the 1648 Peace of Westphalia, which ushered in the era of organized nation-states.

As a consequence, roughly 400,000 Sierra Leonians are internally displaced, 280,000 more have fled to neighboring Guinea, and another 100,000 have fled to Liberia, even as 400,000 Liberians have fled to Sierra Leone. The third largest city in Sierra Leone, Gondama, is a displaced-persons camp. With an additional 600,000 Liberians in Guinea and 250,000 in the Ivory Coast, the borders dividing these four countries have become largely meaningless. Even in quiet zones none of the governments except the Ivory Coast's maintains the schools, bridges, roads, and police forces in a manner necessary for functional sovereignty. The Koranko ethnic group in northeastern Sierra Leone does all its trading in Guinea. Sierra Leonian diamonds are more likely to be sold in Liberia than in Freetown. In the eastern provinces of Sierra Leone you can buy Liberian beer but not the local brand.

In Sierra Leone, as in Guinea, as in the Ivory Coast, as in Ghana, most of the primary rain forest and the secondary bush is being destroyed at an alarming rate. I saw convoys of trucks bearing majestic hardwood trunks to coastal ports. When Sierra Leone achieved its independence, in 1961, as much as 60 percent of the country was primary rain forest. Now 6 percent is. In the Ivory Coast the proportion has fallen from 38 percent to 8 percent. The deforestation has led to soil erosion, which has led to more flooding and more mosquitoes. Virtually everyone in the West African interior has some form of malaria.

Sierra Leone is a microcosm of what is occurring, albeit in a more tempered and gradual manner, throughout West Africa and much of the underdeveloped world: the withering away of central governments, the rise of tribal and regional domains, the unchecked spread of disease, and the growing pervasiveness of war. West Africa is reverting to the Africa of the Victorian atlas. It consists now of a series of coastal trading posts, such as Freetown and Conakry, and an interior that, owing to violence, volatility, and disease, is again becoming, as Graham Greene once observed, "blank" and "unexplored." However, whereas Greene's vision implies a certain romance, as in the somnolent and charmingly seedy Freetown of his celebrated novel *The Heart of the Matter,* it is Thomas Malthus, the philosopher of demographic doomsday, who is now the prophet of West Africa's future. And West Africa's future, eventually, will also be that of most of the rest of the world.

CONSIDER "CHICAGO." I refer not to Chicago, Illinois, but to a slum district of Abidjan, which the young toughs in the area have named after the American city. ("Washington" is another poor section of Abidjan.) Although Sierra Leone is widely regarded as beyond salvage, the Ivory Coast has been considered an African success story, and Abidjan has been called "the Paris of West Africa." Success, however, was built on two artificial factors: the high price of cocoa, of which the Ivory Coast is the world's leading producer, and the talents of a French expatriate community, whose members have helped run the government and the private sector. The expanding cocoa economy made the Ivory Coast a magnet for migrant workers from all over West Africa: between a third and a half of the country's population is now non-Ivorian, and the figure could be as high as 75 percent in Abidjan. During the 1980s cocoa prices fell and the French began to leave. The skyscrapers of the Paris of West Africa are a façade. Perhaps 15 percent of Abidjan's population of three million people live in shantytowns like Chicago and Washington, and the vast majority live in places that are not much better. Not all of these places appear on any of the readily available maps. This is another indication of how political maps are the products of tired conventional wisdom and, in the Ivory Coast's case, of an elite that will ultimately be forced to relinquish power.

Chicago, like more and more of Abidjan, is a slum in the bush: a checkerwork of corrugated zinc roofs and walls made of cardboard and black plastic wrap. It is located in a gully teeming with coconut palms and oil palms, and is ravaged by flooding. Few residents have easy access to electricity, a sewage system, or a clean water supply. The crumbly red laterite earth crawls with foot-long lizards both inside and outside the shacks. Children defecate in a stream filled with garbage and pigs, droning with mosquitoes. In this stream women do the washing. Young unemployed men spend their time drinking beer, palm wine, and gin while gambling on pinball games constructed out of rotting wood and rusty nails. These are the same youths who rob houses in more prosperous Ivorian neighborhoods at night. One man I met, Damba Tesele, came to Chicago from Burkina Faso in 1963. A cook by profession, he has four wives and thirty-two children, not one of whom has made it to high school. He has seen his shanty community destroyed by municipal authorities seven times since coming to the area. Each time he and his neighbors rebuild. Chicago is the latest incarnation.

Fifty-five percent of the Ivory Coast's population is urban, and the proportion is expected to reach 62 percent by 2000. The yearly net population growth is 3.6 percent. This means that the Ivory Coast's 13.5 million people will become 39 million by 2025, when much of the population will consist of urbanized peasants like those of Chicago. But don't count on the Ivory Coast's still existing then. Chicago, which is more indicative of Africa's and the Third World's demographic present—and even more of the future—than any idyllic junglescape of women balancing earthen jugs on their heads, illustrates why the Ivory Coast, once a model of Third World success, is becoming a case study in Third World catastrophe.

President Félix Houphouët-Boigny, who died last December at the age of about ninety, left behind a weak cluster of political parties and a leaden bureaucracy that discourages foreign investment. Because the military is small and the non-Ivorian population large, there is neither an obvious force to maintain order nor a sense of nationhood that would lessen the need for such enforcement. The economy has been shrinking since the mid-1980s. Though the French are working assiduously to preserve stability, the Ivory Coast faces a possibility worse than a coup: an anarchic implosion of criminal violence—an urbanized version of what has already happened in Somalia. Or it may become an African Yugoslavia, but one without ministates to replace the whole.

Because the demographic reality of West Africa is a countryside draining into dense slums by the coast, ultimately the region's rulers will come to reflect the values of these shantytowns. There are signs of this already in Sierra Leone—and in Togo, where the dictator Etienne Eyadema, in power since 1967, was nearly toppled in 1991, not by democrats but by thousands of youths whom the London-based magazine *West Africa* described as "Soweto-like stone-throwing adolescents." Their behavior may herald a regime more brutal than Eyadema's repressive one.

The fragility of these West African "countries" impressed itself on me when I took a series of bush taxis along the Gulf of Guinea, from the Togolese capital of Lomé, across Ghana, to Abidjan. The four-hundred-mile journey required two full days of driving, because of stops at two border crossings and an additional eleven customs stations, at each of which my fellow passengers had their bags searched. I had to change money twice and repeatedly fill in currency-declaration forms. I had to bribe a Togolese immigration official with the equivalent of eighteen dollars before he would agree to put an exit stamp on my passport. Nevertheless, smuggling across these borders is rampant. *The London Observer* has reported that in 1992 the equivalent of $856 million left West Africa for Europe in the form of "hot cash" assumed to be laundered drug money. International cartels have discovered the utility of weak, financially strapped West African regimes.

The more fictitious the actual sovereignty, the more severe border authorities seem to be in trying to prove otherwise. Getting visas for these states can be as hard as crossing their borders. The Washington embassies of Sierra Leone and Guinea—the two poorest nations on earth, according to a 1993 United Nations report on "human development"—asked for letters from my bank (in lieu of prepaid round-trip tickets) and also personal references, in order to prove that I had sufficient means to sustain myself during my visits. I was reminded of my visa and currency hassles while traveling to the communist states of Eastern Europe, particularly East Germany and Czechoslovakia, before those states collapsed.

Ali A. Mazrui, the director of the Institute of Global Cultural Studies at the State University of New York at Binghamton, predicts that West Africa—indeed, the whole continent—is on the verge of large-scale border upheaval. Mazrui writes,

In the 21st century France will be withdrawing from West Africa as she gets increasingly involved in the affairs [of Europe]. France's West African sphere of influence will be filled by Nigeria—a more natural hegemonic power. . . . It will be under those circumstances that Nigeria's own boundaries are likely to expand to incorporate the Republic of Niger (the Hausa link), the Republic of Benin (the Yoruba link) and conceivably Cameroon.

THE FUTURE COULD be more tumultuous, and bloodier, than Mazrui dares to say. France *will* withdraw from former colonies like Benin, Togo, Niger, and the Ivory Coast, where it has been propping up local currencies. It will do so not only because its attention will be diverted to new challenges in Europe and Russia but also because younger French officials lack the older generation's emotional ties to the ex-colonies. However, even as Nigeria attempts to expand, it, too, is likely to split into several pieces. The State Department's Bureau of Intelligence and Research recently made the following points in an analysis of Nigeria:

> Prospects for a transition to civilian rule and democratization are slim. . . . The repressive apparatus of the state security service . . . will be difficult for any future civilian government to control. . . . The country is becoming increasingly ungovernable. . . . Ethnic and regional splits are deepening, a situation made worse by an increase in the number of states from 19 to 30 and a

doubling in the number of local governing authorities; religious cleavages are more serious; Muslim fundamentalism and evangelical Christian militancy are on the rise; and northern Muslim anxiety over southern [Christian] control of the economy is intense . . . the will to keep Nigeria together is now very weak.

Given that oil-rich Nigeria is a bellwether for the region—its population of roughly ninety million equals the populations of all the other West African states combined—it is apparent that Africa faces cataclysms that could make the Ethiopian and Somalian famines pale in comparison. This is especially so because Nigeria's population, including that of its largest city, Lagos, whose crime, pollution, and overcrowding make it the cliché par excellence of Third World urban dysfunction, is set to double during the next twenty-five years, while the country continues to deplete its natural resources.

Part of West Africa's quandary is that although its population belts are horizontal, with habitation densities increasing as one travels south away from the Sahara and toward the tropical abundance of the Atlantic littoral, the borders erected by European colonialists are vertical, and therefore at cross-purposes with demography and topography. Satellite photos depict the same reality I experienced in the bush taxi: the Lomé-Abidjan coastal corridor—indeed, the entire stretch of coast from Abidjan eastward to Lagos—is one burgeoning megalopolis that by any rational economic and geographical standard should constitute a single sovereignty, rather than the five (the Ivory Coast,

Ghana, Togo, Benin, and Nigeria) into which it is currently divided.

As many internal African borders begin to crumble, a more impenetrable boundary is being erected that threatens to isolate the continent as a whole: the wall of disease. Merely to visit West Africa in some degree of safety, I spent about five hundred dollars for a hepatitis B vaccination series and other disease prophylaxis. Africa may today be more dangerous in this regard than it was in 1862, before antibiotics, when the explorer Sir Richard Francis Burton described the health situation on the continent as "deadly, a Golgotha, a Jehannum." Of the approximately twelve million people worldwide whose blood is HIV-positive, eight million are in Africa. In the capital of the Ivory Coast, whose modern road system only helps to spread the disease, 10 percent of the population is HIV-positive. And war and refugee movements help the virus break through to more-remote areas of Africa. Alan Greenberg, M.D., a representative of the Centers for Disease Control in Abidjan, explains that in Africa the HIV virus and tuberculosis are now "fast-forwarding each other." Of the approximately four thousand newly diagnosed tuberculosis patients in Abidjan, 45 percent were also found to be HIV-positive. As African birth rates soar and slums proliferate, some experts worry that viral mutations and hybridizations might, just conceivably, result in a form of the AIDS virus that is easier to catch than the present strain.

It is malaria that is most responsible for the disease wall that threatens to separate Africa and other parts of the Third

World from more-developed regions of the planet in the twenty-first century. Carried by mosquitoes, malaria, unlike AIDS, is easy to catch. Most people in sub-Saharan Africa have recurring bouts of the disease throughout their entire lives, and it is mutating into increasingly deadly forms. "The great gift of Malaria is utter apathy," wrote Sir Richard Burton, accurately portraying the situation in much of the Third World today. Visitors to malaria-afflicted parts of the planet are protected by a new drug, mefloquine, a side effect of which is vivid, even violent, dreams. But a strain of cerebral malaria resistant to mefloquine is now on the offensive. Consequently, defending oneself against malaria in Africa is becoming more and more like defending oneself against violent crime. You engage in "behavior modification": not going out at dusk, wearing mosquito repellent all the time.

And the cities keep growing. I got a general sense of the future while driving from the airport to downtown Conakry, the capital of Guinea. The forty-five-minute journey in heavy traffic was through one never-ending shantytown: a nightmarish Dickensian spectacle to which Dickens himself would never have given credence. The corrugated metal shacks and scabrous walls were coated with black slime. Stores were built out of rusted shipping containers, junked cars, and jumbles of wire mesh. The streets were one long puddle of floating garbage. Mosquitoes and flies were everywhere. Children, many of whom had protruding bellies, seemed as numerous as ants. When the tide went out, dead rats and the skeletons of cars were exposed on the mucky beach. In twenty-eight years

Guinea's population will double if growth goes on at current rates. Hardwood logging continues at a madcap speed, and people flee the Guinean countryside for Conakry. It seemed to me that here, as elsewhere in Africa and the Third World, man is challenging nature far beyond its limits, and nature is now beginning to take its revenge.

AFRICA MAY BE as relevant to the future character of world politics as the Balkans were a hundred years ago, prior to the two Balkan wars and the First World War. Then the threat was the collapse of empires and the birth of nations based solely on tribe. Now the threat is more elemental: *nature unchecked*. Africa's immediate future could be very bad. The coming upheaval, in which foreign embassies are shut down, states collapse, and contact with the outside world takes place through dangerous, disease-ridden coastal trading posts, will loom large in the century we are entering. (Nine of twenty-one U.S. foreign-aid missions to be closed over the next three years are in Africa—a prologue to a consolidation of U.S. embassies themselves.) Precisely because much of Africa is set to go over the edge at a time when the Cold War has ended, when environmental and demographic stress in other parts of the globe is becoming critical, and when the post–First World War system of nation-states—not just in the Balkans but perhaps also in the Middle East—is about to be toppled, Africa suggests what war, borders, and ethnic politics will be like a few decades hence.

To understand the events of the next fifty years, then, one

must understand environmental scarcity, cultural and racial clash, geographic destiny, and the transformation of war. The order in which I have named these is not accidental. Each concept except the first relies partly on the one or ones before it, meaning that the last two—new approaches to mapmaking and to warfare—are the most important. They are also the least understood. I will now look at each idea, drawing upon the work of specialists and also my own travel experiences in various parts of the globe besides Africa, in order to fill in the blanks of a new political atlas.

The Environment as a Hostile Power

FOR A WHILE the media will continue to ascribe riots and other violent upheavals abroad mainly to ethnic and religious conflict. But as these conflicts multiply, it will become apparent that something else is afoot, making more and more places like Nigeria, India, and Brazil ungovernable.

Mention "the environment" or "diminishing natural resources" in foreign-policy circles and you meet a brick wall of skepticism or boredom. To conservatives especially, the very terms seem flaky. Public-policy foundations have contributed to the lack of interest, by funding narrowly focused environmental studies replete with technical jargon which foreign-affairs experts just let pile up on their desks.

It is time to understand "the environment" for what it is: *the* national-security issue of the early twenty-first century. The political and strategic impact of surging populations, spreading disease, deforestation and soil erosion, water depletion, air pollution, and, possibly, rising sea levels in critical, overcrowded regions like the Nile Delta and Bangladesh—developments that will prompt mass migrations and, in turn, incite group conflicts—will be the core foreign-policy challenge from which most others will ultimately emanate, arousing the public and uniting assorted interests left over from the Cold War. In the twenty-first century water will be in dangerously short supply in such diverse locales as Saudi Arabia, Central Asia, and the southwestern United States. A war could erupt between Egypt and Ethiopia over Nile River water. Even in Europe tensions have arisen between Hungary and Slovakia over the damming of the Danube, a classic case of how environmental disputes fuse with ethnic and historical ones. The political scientist and erstwhile Clinton adviser Michael Mandelbaum has said, "We have a foreign policy today in the shape of a doughnut—lots of peripheral interests but nothing at the center." The environment, I will argue, is part of a terrifying array of problems that will define a new threat to our security, filling the hole in Mandelbaum's doughnut and allowing a post–Cold War foreign policy to emerge inexorably by need rather than by design.

OUR COLD WAR foreign policy truly began with George F. Kennan's famous article, signed "X," published in *Foreign Affairs* in July 1947, in which Kennan argued for a "firm and vigilant containment" of a Soviet Union that was imperially, rather than ideologically, motivated. It may be that our post–Cold War foreign policy will one day be seen to have had its beginnings in an even bolder and more detailed piece of written analysis: one that appeared in the journal *International Security*. The article, published in the fall of 1991 by Thomas Fraser Homer-Dixon, who is the head of the Peace and Conflict Studies Program at the University of Toronto, was titled "On the Threshold: Environmental Changes as Causes of Acute Conflict." Homer-Dixon has, more successfully than other analysts, integrated two hither-to separate fields—military-conflict studies and the study of the physical environment.

In Homer-Dixon's view, future wars and civil violence will often arise from scarcities of resources such as water, cropland, forests, and fish. Just as there will be environmentally driven wars and refugee flows, there will be environmentally induced praetorian regimes—or, as he puts it, "hard regimes." Countries with the highest probability of acquiring hard regimes, according to Homer-Dixon, are those that are threatened by a declining resource base yet also have "a history of state [read 'military'] strength." Candidates include Indonesia, Brazil, and, of course, Nigeria. Though each of these nations has exhibited democratizing tendencies of late, Homer-Dixon argues that such tendencies are likely to be superficial "epiphenomena" having nothing to do with long-term processes that include soaring populations and shrinking raw materials. Democracy is problematic; scarcity is more certain.

Indeed, the Saddam Husseins of the future will have more, not fewer, opportunities. In addition to engendering tribal strife, scarcer resources will place a great strain on many peoples who never had much of a democratic or institutional tradition to begin with. Over the next fifty years the earth's population will soar from 5.5 billion to more than 9 billion. Though optimists have hopes for new resource technologies and free-market development in the global village, they fail to note that, as the National Academy of Sciences has pointed out, 95 percent of the population increase will be in the poorest regions of the world, where governments now—just look at Africa—show little ability to function, let alone to implement even marginal improvements. Homer-Dixon writes, ominously, "Neo-Malthusians may underestimate human adaptability in *today's* environmental-social system, but as time passes their analysis may become ever more compelling."

While a minority of the human population will be, as Francis Fukuyama would put it, sufficiently sheltered so as to enter a "post-historical" realm, living in cities and suburbs in which the environment has been mastered and ethnic animosities have been quelled by bourgeois prosperity, an increasingly large number of people will be stuck in history, living in shanty-towns where attempts to rise above poverty, cultural dysfunction, and ethnic strife will be doomed by a lack of water to drink, soil to till, and space to survive in. In the developing world environmental stress will present people with a choice that is increasingly among totalitarianism (as in Iraq), fascist-tending mini-states (as in Serb-held Bosnia), and road-warrior cultures (as in Somalia). Homer-Dixon concludes that "as environmental degradation proceeds, the size of the potential social disruption will increase."

Tad Homer-Dixon is an unlikely Jeremiah. Today a boyish thirty-seven, he grew up amid the sylvan majesty of Vancouver Island, attending private day schools. His speech is calm, perfectly even, and crisply enunciated. There is nothing in his background or manner that would indicate a bent toward pessimism. A Canadian Anglican who spends his summers canoeing on the lakes of northern Ontario, and who talks about the benign mountains, black bears, and Douglas firs of his youth, he is the opposite of the intellectually severe neoconservative, the kind at home with conflict scenarios. Nor is he an environmentalist who opposes development. "My father was a logger who thought about ecologically safe forestry before others," he says. "He logged, planted, logged, and planted. He got out of the business just as the issue was being polarized by environmentalists. They hate changed ecosystems. But human beings, just by carrying seeds around, change the natural world." As an only child whose playground was a virtually untouched wilderness and seacoast, Homer-Dixon has a familiarity with the natural world that permits him to see a reality that most policy analysts—children of suburbia and city streets—are blind to.

"We need to bring nature back in," he argues. "We have to stop separating politics from the physical world—the climate, public health, and the environment." Quoting Daniel Deudney, another pioneering expert on the security aspects of the environment, Homer-Dixon says that "for too long we've been pris-

oners of 'social-social' theory, which assumes there are only social causes for social and political changes, rather than natural
causes, too. This social-social mentality emerged with the Industrial Revolution, which separated us from nature. But nature is coming back with a vengeance, tied to population
growth. It will have incredible security implications.

"Think of a stretch limo in the potholed streets of New York
City, where homeless beggars live. Inside the limo are the air-
conditioned postindustrial regions of North America, Europe,
the emerging Pacific Rim, and a few other isolated places, with
their trade summitry and computer-information highways.
Outside is the rest of mankind, going in a completely different
direction."

WE ARE ENTERING a bifurcated world. Part of the globe is in-
habited by Hegel's and Fukuyama's Last Man, healthy, well fed,
and pampered by technology. The other, larger, part is inhab-
ited by Hobbes's First Man, condemned to a life that is "poor,
nasty, brutish, and short." Although both parts will be threatened by environmental stress, the Last Man will be able to master it; the First Man will not.

The Last Man will adjust to the loss of underground water
tables in the western United States. He will build dikes to save
Cape Hatteras and the Chesapeake beaches from rising sea levels, even as the Maldive Islands, off the coast of India, sink into
oblivion, and the shorelines of Egypt, Bangladesh, and Southeast Asia recede, driving tens of millions of people inland

where there is no room for them, and thus sharpening ethnic divisions.

Homer-Dixon points to a world map of soil degradation in his Toronto office. "The darker the map color, the worse the degradation," he explains. The West African coast, the Middle East, the Indian subcontinent, China, and Central America have the darkest shades, signifying all manner of degradation, related to winds, chemicals, and water problems. "The worst degradation is generally where the population is highest. The population is generally highest where the soil is the best. So we're degrading earth's best soil."

China, in Homer-Dixon's view, is the quintessential example of environmental degradation. Its current economic "success" masks deeper problems. "China's fourteen percent growth rate does not mean it's going to be a world power. It means that coastal China, where the economic growth is taking place, is joining the rest of the Pacific Rim. The disparity with inland China is intensifying." Referring to the environmental research of his colleague, the Czech-born ecologist Vaclav Smil, Homer-Dixon explains how the per capita availability of arable land in interior China has rapidly declined at the same time that the quality of that land has been destroyed by deforestation, loss of topsoil, and salinization. He mentions the loss and contamination of water supplies, the exhaustion of wells, the plugging of irrigation systems and reservoirs with eroded silt, and a population of 1.54 billion by the year 2025: it is a misconception that China has gotten its population under control. Large-scale population movements are under way, from inland

China to coastal China and from villages to cities, leading to a crime surge like the one in Africa and to growing regional disparities and conflicts in a land with a strong tradition of warlordism and a weak tradition of central government—again as in Africa. "We will probably see the center challenged and fractured, and China will not remain the same on the map," Homer-Dixon says.

Environmental scarcity will inflame existing hatreds and affect power relationships, at which we now look.

SKINHEAD COSSACKS, *JUJU* WARRIORS

IN THE SUMMER 1993 issue of *Foreign Affairs,* Samuel P. Huntington, of Harvard's Olin Institute for Strategic Studies, published a thought-provoking article called "The Clash of Civilizations?" The world, he argues, has been moving during the course of this century from nation-state conflict to ideological conflict to, finally, cultural conflict. I would add that as refugee flows increase and as peasants continue migrating to cities around the world—turning them into sprawling villages—national borders will mean less, even as more power will fall into the hands of less educated, less sophisticated groups. In the eyes of these uneducated but newly empowered millions, the real borders are the most tangible and intractable ones: those of culture and tribe. Huntington writes, "First, differences among civilizations are not only real; they are basic," involving, among other things, history, language, and religion. "Second . . . interactions between peoples of different civilizations are increasing; these increasing interactions intensify civilization consciousness." Economic modernization is not necessarily a panacea, since it fuels individual and group ambitions while weakening traditional loyalties to the state. It is worth noting, for example, that it is precisely the wealthiest and fastest-developing city in India, Bombay, that has seen the worst intercommunal violence between Hindus and Muslims. Consider that Indian cities, like African and Chinese ones, are ecological time bombs—Delhi and Calcutta, and also Beijing, suffer the worst air quality of any cities in the world—and it is apparent how surging populations, environmental degradation, and ethnic conflict are deeply related.

Huntington points to interlocking conflicts among Hindu, Muslim, Slavic Orthodox, Western, Japanese, Confucian, Latin American, and possibly African civilizations: for instance, Hindus clashing with Muslims in India, Turkic Muslims clashing with Slavic Orthodox Russians in Central Asian cities, the West clashing with Asia. (Even in the United States, African-Americans find themselves besieged by an influx of competing Latinos.) Whatever the laws, refugees find a way to crash official borders, bringing their passions with them, meaning that Europe and the United States will be weakened by cultural disputes.

Because Huntington's brush is broad, his specifics are vulnerable to attack. In a rebuttal of Huntington's argument the

Johns Hopkins professor Fouad Ajami, a Lebanese-born Shi'ite who certainly knows the world beyond suburbia, writes in the September-October 1993 issue of *Foreign Affairs,*

> The world of Islam divides and subdivides. The battle lines in the Caucasus . . . are not coextensive with civilizational fault lines. The lines follow the interests of states. Where Huntington sees a civilizational duel between Armenia and Azerbaijan, the Iranian state has cast religious zeal . . . to the wind . . . in that battle the Iranians have tilted toward Christian Armenia.

True, Huntington's hypothesized war between Islam and Orthodox Christianity is not borne out by the alliance network in the Caucasus. But that is only because he has misidentified *which* cultural war is occurring there. A recent visit to Azerbaijan made clear to me that Azeri Turks, the world's most secular Shi'ite Muslims, see their cultural identity in terms not of religion but of their Turkic race. The Armenians, likewise, fight the Azeris not because the latter are Muslims but because they are Turks, related to the same Turks who massacred Armenians in 1915. Turkic culture (secular and based on languages employing a Latin script) is battling Iranian culture (religiously militant as defined by Tehran, and wedded to an Arabic script) across the whole swath of Central Asia and the Caucasus. The Armenians are, therefore, natural allies of their fellow Indo-Europeans the Iranians.

Huntington is correct that the Caucasus is a flashpoint of

cultural and racial war. But, as Ajami observes, Huntington's plate tectonics are too simple. Two months of recent travel throughout Turkey revealed to me that although the Turks are developing a deep distrust, bordering on hatred, of fellow-Muslim Iran, they are also, especially in the shantytowns that are coming to dominate Turkish public opinion, revising their group identity, increasingly seeing themselves as Muslims being deserted by a West that does little to help besieged Muslims in Bosnia and that attacks Turkish Muslims in the streets of Germany.

In other words, the Balkans, a powder keg for nation-state war at the beginning of the twentieth century, could be a powder keg for cultural war at the turn of the twenty-first: between Orthodox Christianity (represented by the Serbs and a classic Byzantine configuration of Greeks, Russians, and Romanians) and the House of Islam. Yet in the Caucasus that House of Islam is falling into a clash between Turkic and Iranian civilizations. Ajami asserts that this very subdivision, not to mention all the divisions within the Arab world, indicates that the West, including the United States, is not threatened by Huntington's scenario. As the Gulf War demonstrated, the West has proved capable of playing one part of the House of Islam against another.

True. However, whether he is aware of it or not, Ajami is describing a world even more dangerous than the one Huntington envisions, especially when one takes into account Homer-Dixon's research on environmental scarcity. Outside the stretch limo would be a rundown, crowded planet of skinhead Cossacks and *juju* warriors, influenced by the worst refuse of Western pop culture and ancient tribal hatreds, and battling over scraps of overused earth in guerrilla conflicts that ripple across continents and intersect in no discernible pattern— meaning there's no easy-to-define threat. Kennan's world of one adversary seems as distant as the world of Herodotus.

Most people believe that the political earth since 1989 has undergone immense change. But it is minor compared with what is yet to come. The breaking apart and remaking of the atlas is only now beginning. The crack-up of the Soviet empire and the coming end of the Arab-Israeli military confrontation are merely prologues to the really big changes that lie ahead. Michael Vlahos, a long-range thinker for the U.S. Navy, warns, "We are not in charge of the environment and the world is not following us. It is going in many directions. Do not assume that democratic capitalism is the last word in human social evolution."

Before addressing the questions of maps and of warfare, I want to take a closer look at the interaction of religion, culture, demographic shifts, and the distribution of natural resources in a specific area of the world: the Middle East.

THE PAST IS DEAD

BUILT ON STEEP, muddy hills, the shantytowns of Ankara, the Turkish capital, exude visual drama. Altindag, or "Golden Mountain," is a pyramid of dreams, fashioned from cinder blocks and corrugated iron, rising as though each shack were built on top of another, all reaching awkwardly and painfully toward heaven—the heaven of wealthier Turks who live elsewhere in the city. Nowhere else on the planet have I found such a poignant architectural symbol of man's striving, with gaps in house walls plugged with rusted cans, and leeks and onions growing on verandas assembled from planks of rotting wood. For reasons that I will explain, the Turkish shacktown is a psychological universe away from the African one.

To see the twenty-first century truly, one's eyes must learn a different set of aesthetics. One must reject the overly stylized images of travel magazines, with their inviting photographs of exotic villages and glamorous downtowns. There are far too many millions whose dreams are more vulgar, more real— whose raw energies and desires will overwhelm the visions of the elites, remaking the future into something frighteningly new. But in Turkey I learned that shantytowns are not all bad.

Slum quarters in Abidjan terrify and repel the outsider. In Turkey it is the opposite. The closer I got to Golden Mountain the better it looked, and the safer I felt. I had fifteen hundred dollars' worth of Turkish lira in one pocket and a thousand dollars in traveler's checks in the other, yet I felt no fear. Golden Mountain was a real neighborhood. The inside of one house told the story: the architectural bedlam of cinder block and sheet metal and cardboard walls was deceiving. Inside was a *home*—order, that is, bespeaking dignity. I saw a working refrigerator, a television, a wall cabinet with a few books and lots of family pictures, a few plants by a window, and a stove.

Though the streets become rivers of mud when it rains, the floors inside this house were spotless.

Other houses were like this too. Schoolchildren ran along with briefcases strapped to their backs, trucks delivered cooking gas, a few men sat inside a café sipping tea. One man sipped beer. Alcohol is easy to obtain in Turkey, a secular state where 99 percent of the population is Muslim. Yet there is little problem of alcoholism. Crime against persons is infinitesimal. Poverty and illiteracy are watered-down versions of what obtains in Algeria and Egypt (to say nothing of West Africa), making it that much harder for religious extremists to gain a foothold.

My point in bringing up a rather wholesome, crime-free slum is this: its existence demonstrates how formidable is the fabric of which Turkish Muslim culture is made. A culture this strong has the potential to dominate the Middle East once again. Slums are litmus tests for innate cultural strengths and weaknesses. Those peoples whose cultures can harbor extensive slum life without decomposing will be, relatively speaking, the future's winners. Those whose cultures cannot will be the future's victims. Slums—in the sociological sense—do not exist in Turkish cities. The mortar between people and family groups is stronger here than in Africa. Resurgent Islam and Turkic cultural identity have produced a civilization with natural muscle tone. Turks, history's perennial nomads, take disruption in stride.

The future of the Middle East is quietly being written inside the heads of Golden Mountain's inhabitants. Think of an Ottoman military encampment on the eve of the destruction of Greek Constantinople in 1453. That is Golden Mountain. "We brought the village here. But in the village we worked harder— in the field, all day. So we couldn't fast during [the holy month of] Ramadan. Here we fast. Here we are more religious." Aishe Tanrıkulu, along with half a dozen other women, was stuffing rice into vine leaves from a crude plastic bowl. She asked me to join her under the shade of a piece of sheet metal. Each of these women had her hair covered by a kerchief. In the city they were encountering television for the first time. "We are traditional, religious people. The programs offend us," Aishe said. Another woman complained about the schools. Though her children had educational options unavailable in the village, they had to compete with wealthier, secular Turks. "The kids from rich families with connections—they get all the places." More opportunities, more tensions, in other words.

My guidebook to Golden Mountain was an untypical one: *Tales from the Garbage Hills,* a brutally realistic novel by a Turkish writer, Latife Tekin, about life in the shantytowns, which in Turkey are called *gecekondus* ("built in a night"). "He listened to the earth and wept unceasingly for water, for work and for the cure of the illnesses spread by the garbage and the factory waste," Tekin writes. In the most revealing passage of *Tales from the Garbage Hills* the squatters are told "about a certain 'Ottoman Empire' . . . that where they now lived there had once been an empire of this name." This history "confounded" the squatters. It was the first they had heard of it. Though one of them knew "that his grandfather and his dog died fighting the

Greeks," nationalism and an encompassing sense of Turkish history are the province of the Turkish middle and upper classes, and of foreigners like me who feel required to have a notion of "Turkey."

But what did the Golden Mountain squatters know about the armies of Turkish migrants that had come before their own—namely, Seljuks and Ottomans? For these recently urbanized peasants, and their counterparts in Africa, the Arab world, India, and so many other places, the world is new, to adapt V. S. Naipaul's phrase. As Naipaul wrote of urban refugees in *India: A Wounded Civilization,* "They saw themselves at the beginning of things: unaccommodated men making a claim on their land for the first time, and out of chaos evolving their own philosophy of community and self-help. For them the past was dead; they had left it behind in the villages."

Everywhere in the developing world at the turn of the twenty-first century these new men and women, rushing into the cities, are remaking civilizations and redefining their identities in terms of religion and tribal ethnicity which do not coincide with the borders of existing states.

IN TURKEY SEVERAL THINGS are happening at once. In 1980, 44 percent of Turks lived in cities; in 1990 it was 61 percent. By the year 2000 the figure is expected to be 67 percent. Villages are emptying out as concentric rings of *gecekondu* developments grow around Turkish cities. This is the real political and demographic revolution in Turkey and elsewhere, and foreign correspondents usually don't write about it.

Whereas rural poverty is age-old and almost a "normal" part of the social fabric, urban poverty is socially destabilizing. As Iran has shown, Islamic extremism is the psychological defense mechanism of many urbanized peasants threatened with the loss of traditions in pseudomodern cities where their values are under attack, where basic services like water and electricity are unavailable, and where they are assaulted by a physically unhealthy environment. The American ethnologist and Orientalist Carleton Stevens Coon wrote in 1951 that Islam "has made possible the optimum survival and happiness of millions of human beings in an increasingly impoverished environment over a fourteen-hundred-year period." Beyond its stark, clearly articulated message, Islam's very militancy makes it attractive to the downtrodden. It is the one religion that is prepared to *fight*. A political era driven by environmental stress, increased cultural sensitivity, unregulated urbanization, and refugee migrations is an era divinely created for the spread and intensification of Islam, already the world's fastest-growing religion. (Though Islam is spreading in West Africa, it is being hobbled by syncretization with animism: this makes new converts less apt to become anti-Western extremists, but it also makes for a weakened version of the faith, which is less effective as an antidote to crime.)

In Turkey, however, Islam is painfully and awkwardly forging a consensus with modernization, a trend that is less apparent in the Arab and Persian worlds (and virtually invisible in Africa). In Iran the oil boom—because it put development and urbanization on a fast track, making the culture shock more intense—fueled the 1978 Islamic Revolution. But Turkey, unlike Iran and the Arab world, has little oil. Therefore its development and urbanization have been more gradual. Islamists have been integrated into the parliamentary system for decades. The tensions I noticed in Golden Mountain are natural, creative ones: the kind immigrants face the world over. While the world has focused on religious perversity in Algeria, a nation rich in natural gas, and in Egypt, parts of whose capital city, Cairo, evince worse crowding than I have seen even in Calcutta, Turkey has been living through the Muslim equivalent of the Protestant Reformation.

Resource distribution is strengthening Turks in another way vis-à-vis Arabs and Persians. Turks may have little oil, but their Anatolian heartland has lots of water—the most important fluid of the twenty-first century. Turkey's Southeast Anatolia Project, involving twenty-two major dams and irrigation systems, is impounding the waters of the Tigris and Euphrates Rivers. Much of the water that Arabs and perhaps Israelis will need to drink in the future is controlled by Turks. The project's centerpiece is the mile-wide, sixteen-story Atatürk Dam, upon which are emblazoned the words of modern Turkey's founder: "*Ne Mutlu Turkum Diyene*" ("Lucky is the one who is a Turk").

Unlike Egypt's Aswan High Dam, on the Nile, and Syria's Revolution Dam, on the Euphrates, both of which were built largely by Russians, the Atatürk Dam is a predominantly Turkish affair, with Turkish engineers and companies in charge. On a recent visit my eyes took in the immaculate offices and their gardens, the high-voltage electric grids and phone switching stations, the dizzying sweep of giant humming transformers, the poured-concrete spillways, and the prim unfolding suburbia, complete with schools, for dam employees. The emerging power of the Turks was palpable.

Erduhan Bayindir, the site manager at the dam, told me that "while oil can be shipped abroad to enrich only elites, water has to be spread more evenly within the society. . . . It is true, we can stop the flow of water into Syria and Iraq for up to eight months without the same water overflowing our dams, in order to regulate their political behavior."

Power is certainly moving north in the Middle East, from the oil fields of Dhahran, on the Persian Gulf, to the water plain of Harran, in southern Anatolia—near the site of the Atatürk Dam. But will the nation-state of Turkey, as presently constituted, be the inheritor of this wealth?

I very much doubt it.

THE LIES OF MAPMAKERS

WHEREAS WEST AFRICA represents the least stable part of political reality outside Homer-Dixon's stretch limo, Turkey, an organic outgrowth of two Turkish empires that ruled Anatolia for 850 years, has been among the most stable. Turkey's borders were established not by colonial powers but in a war of independence, in the early 1920s. Kemal Atatürk provided Turkey with a secular nation-building myth that most Arab and African states, burdened by artificially drawn borders, lack. That lack will leave many Arab states defenseless against a wave of Islam that will eat away at their legitimacy and frontiers in coming years. Yet even as regards Turkey, maps deceive.

It is not only African shantytowns that don't appear on urban maps. Many shantytowns in Turkey and elsewhere are also missing—as are the considerable territories controlled by guerrilla armies and urban mafias. Traveling with Eritrean guerrillas in what, according to the map, was northern Ethiopia, traveling in "northern Iraq" with Kurdish guerrillas, and staying in a hotel in the Caucasus controlled by a local mafia—to say nothing of my experiences in West Africa—led me to develop a healthy skepticism toward maps, which, I began to realize, create a conceptual barrier that prevents us from comprehending the political crack-up just beginning to occur worldwide.

Consider the map of the world, with its 190 or so countries, each signified by a bold and uniform color: this map, with which all of us have grown up, is generally an invention of modernism, specifically of European colonialism. Modernism, in the sense of which I speak, began with the rise of nation-states in Europe and was confirmed by the death of feudalism at the end of the Thirty Years' War—an event that was interposed between the Renaissance and the Enlightenment, which together gave birth to modern science. People were suddenly flush with an enthusiasm to categorize, to define. The map, based on scientific techniques of measurement, offered a way to classify new national organisms, making a jigsaw puzzle of neat pieces without transition zones between them. "Frontier" is itself a modern concept that didn't exist in the feudal mind. And as European nations carved out far-flung domains at the same time that print technology was making the reproduction of maps cheaper, cartography came into its own as a way of creating facts by ordering the way we look at the world.

In his book *Imagined Communities: Reflections on the Origin and Spread of Nationalism,* Benedict Anderson, of Cornell University, demonstrates that the map enabled colonialists to think about their holdings in terms of a "totalizing classificatory grid. . . . It was bounded, determinate, and therefore—in principle—countable." To the colonialist, country maps were the equivalent of an accountant's ledger books. Maps, Anderson explains, "shaped the grammar" that would make possible such questionable concepts as Iraq, Indonesia, Sierra Leone, and Nigeria. The state, recall, is a purely Western notion, one that until the twentieth century applied to countries covering only 3 percent of the earth's land area. Nor is the evidence compelling that the state, as a governing ideal, can be successfully transported to areas outside the industrialized world. Even the United States of America, in the words of one of our best living poets, Gary Snyder, consists of "arbitrary and inaccurate impositions on what is really here."

Yet this inflexible, artificial reality staggers on, not only in the United Nations but in various geographic and travel publications (themselves by-products of an age of elite touring which colonialism made possible) that still report on and photograph the world according to "country." Newspapers, this magazine, and this writer are not innocent of the tendency.

According to the map, the great hydropower complex emblemized by the Atatürk Dam is situated in Turkey. Forget the map. This southeastern region of Turkey is populated almost completely by Kurds. About half of the world's twenty million Kurds live in "Turkey." The Kurds are predominant in an ellipse of territory that overlaps not only with Turkey but also with Iraq, Iran, Syria, and the former Soviet Union. The Western-enforced Kurdish enclave in northern Iraq, a consequence of the 1991 Gulf War, has already exposed the fictitious nature of that supposed nation-state.

On a recent visit to the Turkish-Iranian border, it occurred to me what a risky idea the nation-state is. Here I was on the legal fault line between two clashing civilizations, Turkic and Iranian. Yet the reality was more subtle: as in West Africa, the border was porous and smuggling abounded, but here the people doing the smuggling, on both sides of the border, were Kurds. In such a moonscape, over which peoples have migrated and settled in patterns that obliterate borders, the end of the Cold War will bring on a cruel process of natural selection among existing states. No longer will these states be so firmly propped up by the West or the Soviet Union. Because the Kurds overlap with nearly everybody in the Middle East, on account of their being cheated out of a state in the post–First World War peace treaties, they are emerging, in effect, as *the* natural selector—the ultimate reality check. They have destabilized Iraq and may continue to disrupt states that do not offer them adequate breathing space, while strengthening states that do.

Because the Turks, owing to their water resources, their growing economy, and the social cohesion evinced by the most crime-free slums I have encountered, are on the verge of big-power status, and because the ten million Kurds within Turkey threaten that status, the outcome of the Turkish-Kurdish dispute will be more critical to the future of the Middle East than the eventual outcome of the recent Israeli-Palestinian agreement.

AMERICA'S FASCINATION WITH the Israeli-Palestinian issue, coupled with its lack of interest in the Turkish-Kurdish one, is a function of its own domestic and ethnic obsessions, not of the cartographic reality that is about to transform the Middle East. The diplomatic process involving Israelis and Palestinians will, I believe, have little effect on the early- and mid-twenty-first-century map of the region. Israel, with a 6.6 percent economic growth rate based increasingly on high-tech exports, is about to enter Homer-Dixon's stretch limo, fortified by a well-defined political community that is an organic outgrowth of history and ethnicity. Like prosperous and peaceful Japan on the one hand, and war-torn and poverty-wracked Armenia on the other, Israel is a classic national-ethnic organism. Much of the Arab world, however, will undergo alteration, as Islam spreads across artificial frontiers, fueled by mass migrations into the cities and a soaring birth rate of more than 3.2 percent. Seventy percent of the Arab population has been born since 1970—youths with little historical memory of anticolonial independence struggles, postcolonial attempts at nation-building, or any of the Arab-Israeli wars. The most distant recollection of these youths will be the West's humiliation of colonially invented Iraq in 1991. Today seventeen out of twenty-two Arab states have a declining gross national product; in the next twenty years, at current growth rates, the population of many Arab countries will double. These states, like most African ones, will be ungovernable through conventional secular ideologies. The Middle East analyst Christine M. Helms explains,

> Declaring Arab nationalism "bankrupt," the political "disinherited" are not rationalizing the failure of Arabism . . . or reformulating it. Alternative solutions are not contemplated. They have simply opted for the political paradigm at the other end of the political spectrum with which they are familiar—Islam.

Like the borders of West Africa, the colonial borders of Syria, Iraq, Jordan, Algeria, and other Arab states are often contrary to cultural and political reality. As state control mechanisms wither in the face of environmental and demographic stress, "hard" Islamic city-states or shantytown-states are likely to emerge. The fiction that the impoverished city of Algiers, on the Mediterranean, controls Tamanrasset, deep in the Algerian Sahara, cannot obtain forever. Whatever the outcome of the peace process, Israel is destined to be a Jewish ethnic fortress amid a vast and volatile realm of Islam. In that realm, the violent youth culture of the Gaza shantytowns may be indicative of the coming era.

The destiny of Turks and Kurds is far less certain, but far more relevant to the kind of map that will explain our future world. The Kurds suggest a geographic reality that cannot be shown in two-dimensional space. The issue in Turkey is not simply a matter of giving autonomy or even independence to Kurds in the southeast. This isn't the Balkans or the Caucasus, where regions are merely subdividing into smaller units, Abkhazia breaking off from Georgia, and so on. Federalism is not the answer. Kurds are found everywhere in Turkey, including the shanty districts of Istanbul and Ankara. Turkey's problem is that its Anatolian land mass is the home of two cultures and languages, Turkish and Kurdish. Identity in Turkey, as in India, Africa, and elsewhere, is more complex and subtle than conventional cartography can display.

A New Kind of War

TO APPRECIATE FULLY the political and cartographic implications of postmodernism—an epoch of themeless juxtapositions, in which the classificatory grid of nation-states is going to be replaced by a jagged-glass pattern of city-states, shanty-states, nebulous and anarchic regionalisms—it is necessary to consider, finally, the whole question of war.

"Oh, what a relief to fight, to fight enemies who defend themselves, enemies who are awake!" André Malraux wrote in *Man's Fate.* I cannot think of a more suitable battle cry for many combatants in the early decades of the twenty-first century. The intense savagery of the fighting in such diverse cultural settings as Liberia, Bosnia, the Caucasus, and Sri Lanka—to say nothing of what obtains in American inner cities—indicates something very troubling that those of us inside the stretch limo, concerned with issues like middle-class entitlements and the future of interactive cable television, lack the stomach to contemplate. It is this: a large number of people on this planet, to whom the comfort and stability of a middle-class life is utterly unknown, find war and a barracks existence a step up rather than a step down.

"Just as it makes no sense to ask 'why people eat' or 'what they sleep for,' " writes Martin van Creveld, a military historian at the Hebrew University in Jerusalem, in *The Transformation of War,* "so fighting in many ways is not a means but an end. Throughout history, for every person who has expressed his horror of war there is another who found in it the most marvelous of all the experiences that are vouchsafed to man, even to the point that he later spent a lifetime boring his descendants by recounting his exploits." When I asked Pentagon officials about the nature of war in the twenty-first century, the answer I frequently got was "Read van Creveld." The top brass are enamored of this historian not because his writings justify their existence but, rather, the opposite: van Creveld warns them that huge state military machines like the Pentagon's are dinosaurs about to go extinct, and that something far more terrible awaits us.

The degree to which van Creveld's *Transformation of War* complements Homer-Dixon's work on the environment, Huntington's thoughts on cultural clash, my own realizations in traveling by foot, bus, and bush taxi in more than sixty countries, and America's sobering comeuppances in intractable-culture zones like Haiti and Somalia is startling. The book begins by demolishing the notion that men don't like to fight. "By compelling the senses to focus themselves on the here and now," van Creveld writes, war "can cause a man to take his leave of them." As anybody who has had experience with Chetniks in Serbia, "technicals" in Somalia, Tontons Macoutes in Haiti, or soldiers in Sierra Leone can tell you, in places where the Western Enlightenment has not penetrated and where there has always been mass poverty, people find liberation in violence. In Afghanistan and elsewhere, I vicariously experienced this phenomenon: worrying about mines and ambushes frees you from worrying about mundane details of daily existence. If my own experience is too subjective, there is a wealth of data showing the sheer frequency of war, especially in the developing world since the Second World War. Physical aggression is a part of being human. Only when people attain a certain economic, educational, and cultural standard is this trait tranquilized. In light of the fact that 95 percent of the earth's population growth will be in the poorest areas of the globe, the question is not whether there will be war (there will be a lot of it) but what kind of war. And who will fight whom?

Debunking the great military strategist Carl von Clause-witz, van Creveld, who may be the most original thinker on war since that early-nineteenth-century Prussian, writes, "Clause-witz's ideas . . . were wholly rooted in the fact that, ever since 1648, war had been waged overwhelmingly by states." But, as van Creveld explains, the period of nation-states and, therefore, of state conflict is now ending, and with it the clear "threefold division into government, army, and people" which state-directed wars enforce. Thus, to see the future, the first step is to look back to the past immediately prior to the birth of mod-ernism—the wars in medieval Europe which began during the Reformation and reached their culmination in the Thirty Years' War.

Van Creveld writes,

> In all these struggles political, social, economic, and re-ligious motives were hopelessly entangled. Since this was an age when armies consisted of mercenaries, all were also attended by swarms of military entrepre-neurs. . . . Many of them paid little but lip service to the organizations for whom they had contracted to fight. Instead, they robbed the countryside on their own be-half. . . .
>
> Given such conditions, any fine distinctions . . . be-tween armies on the one hand and peoples on the

other were bound to break down. Engulfed by war, civilians suffered terrible atrocities.

BACK THEN, IN other words, there was no "politics" as we have come to understand the term, just as there is less and less "politics" today in Liberia, Sierra Leone, Somalia, Sri Lanka, the Balkans, and the Caucasus, among other places.

Because, as van Creveld notes, the radius of trust within tribal societies is narrowed to one's immediate family and guerrilla comrades, truces arranged with one Bosnian commander, say, may be broken immediately by another Bosnian commander. The plethora of short-lived cease-fires in the Balkans and the Caucasus constitute proof that we are no longer in a world where the old rules of state warfare apply. More evidence is provided by the destruction of medieval monuments in the Croatian port of Dubrovnik: when cultures, rather than states, fight, then cultural and religious monuments are weapons of war, making them fair game.

Also, war-making entities will no longer be restricted to a specific territory. Loose and shadowy organisms such as Islamic terrorist organizations suggest why borders will mean increasingly little and sedimentary layers of tribalistic identity and control will mean more. "From the vantage point of the present, there appears every prospect that religious . . . fanaticisms will play a larger role in the motivation of armed conflict" in the West than at any time "for the last 300 years," van Creveld writes. This is why analysts like Michael Vlahos are closely monitoring religious cults. Vlahos says, "An ideology that challenges us may not take familiar form, like the old Nazis or Commies. It may not even engage us initially in ways that fit old threat markings." Van Creveld concludes, "Armed conflict will be waged by men on earth, not robots in space. It will have more in common with the struggles of primitive tribes than with large-scale conventional war." While another military historian, John Keegan, in his book *A History of Warfare,* draws a more benign portrait of primitive man, it is important to point out that what van Creveld really means is *re-primitivized* man: warrior societies operating at a time of unprecedented resource scarcity and planetary overcrowding.

Van Creveld's pre-Westphalian vision of worldwide low-intensity conflict is not a superficial "back to the future" scenario. First of all, technology will be used toward primitive ends. In Liberia the guerrilla leader Prince Johnson didn't just cut off the ears of President Samuel Doe before Doe was tortured to death in 1990—Johnson made a video of it, which has circulated throughout West Africa. In December 1992, when plotters of a failed coup against the Strasser regime in Sierra Leone had their ears cut off at Freetown's Hamilton Beach prior to being killed, it was seen by many to be a copycat execution. Considering, as I've explained earlier, that the Strasser regime is not really a government and that Sierra Leone is not really a nation-state, listen closely to van Creveld: "Once the legal monopoly of armed force, long claimed by the state, is wrested out of its hands, existing distinctions between war and crime will break down much as is already the case today in . . . Lebanon, Sri Lanka, El Salvador, Peru, or Colombia."

If crime and war become indistinguishable, then "national defense" may in the future be viewed as a local concept. As crime continues to grow in our cities and the ability of state governments and criminal-justice systems to protect their citizens diminishes, urban crime may, according to van Creveld, "develop into low-intensity conflict by coalescing along racial, religious, social, and political lines." As small-scale violence multiplies at home and abroad, state armies will continue to shrink, being gradually replaced by a booming private security business, as in West Africa, and by urban mafias, especially in the former communist world, who may be better equipped than municipal police forces to grant physical protection to local inhabitants.

Future wars will be those of communal survival, aggravated or, in many cases, caused by environmental scarcity. These wars will be subnational, meaning that it will be hard for states and local governments to protect their own citizens physically. This is how many states will ultimately die. As state power fades—and with it the state's ability to help weaker groups within society, not to mention other states—peoples and cultures around the world will be thrown back upon their own strengths and weaknesses, with fewer equalizing mechanisms to protect them. Whereas the distant future will probably see the emergence of a racially hybrid, globalized man, the coming decades will see us more aware of our differences than of our similarities. To the average person, political values will mean less, personal security more. The belief that we are all equal is liable to be replaced by the overriding obsession of the ancient Greek travelers: Why the differences between peoples?

THE LAST MAP

IN *Geography and the Human Spirit,* Anne Buttimer, a professor at University College, Dublin, recalls the work of an early-nineteenth-century German geographer, Carl Ritter, whose work implied "a divine plan for humanity" based on regionalism and a constant, living flow of forms. The map of the future, to the extent that a map is even possible, will represent a perverse twisting of Ritter's vision. Imagine cartography in three dimensions, as if in a hologram. In this hologram would be the overlapping sediments of group and other identities atop the merely two-dimensional color markings of city-states and the remaining nations, themselves confused in places by shadowy tentacles, hovering overhead, indicating the power of drug cartels, mafias, and private security agencies. Instead of borders, there would be moving "centers" of power, as in the Middle Ages. Many of these layers would be in motion. Replacing fixed and abrupt lines on a flat space would be a shifting pattern of buffer entities, like the Kurdish and Azeri buffer entities between Turkey and Iran, the Turkic Uighur buffer entity between Central Asia and Inner China (itself distinct from coastal China), and the Latino buffer entity replacing a precise U.S.-

Mexican border. To this protean cartographic hologram one must add other factors, such as migrations of populations, explosions of birth rates, vectors of disease. Henceforward the map of the world will never be static. This future map—in a sense, the "Last Map"—will be an ever-mutating representation of chaos.

The Indian subcontinent offers examples of what is happening. For different reasons, both India and Pakistan are increasingly dysfunctional. The argument over democracy in these places is less and less relevant to the larger issue of governability. In India's case the question arises, Is one unwieldy bureaucracy in New Delhi the best available mechanism for promoting the lives of 866 million people of diverse languages, religions, and ethnic groups? In 1950, when the Indian population was much less than half as large and nation-building idealism was still strong, the argument for democracy was more impressive than it is now. Given that in 2025 India's population could be close to 1.5 billion, that much of its economy rests on a shrinking natural-resource base, including dramatically declining water levels, and that communal violence and urbanization are spiraling upward, it is difficult to imagine that the Indian state will survive the next century. India's oft-trumpeted Green Revolution has been achieved by overworking its croplands and depleting its watershed. Norman Myers, a British development consultant, worries that Indians have "been feeding themselves today by borrowing against their children's food sources."

Pakistan's problem is more basic still: like much of Africa, the country makes no geographic or demographic sense. It was founded as a homeland for the Muslims of the subcontinent, yet there are more subcontinental Muslims outside Pakistan than within it. Like Yugoslavia, Pakistan is a patchwork of ethnic groups, increasingly in violent conflict with one another. While the Western media gushes over the fact that the country has a woman Prime Minister, Benazir Bhutto, Karachi is becoming a subcontinental version of Lagos. In eight visits to Pakistan, I have never gotten a sense of a cohesive national identity. With as much as 65 percent of its land dependent on intensive irrigation, with wide-scale deforestation, and with a yearly population growth of 2.7 percent (which ensures that the amount of cultivated land per rural inhabitant will plummet), Pakistan is becoming a more and more desperate place. As irrigation in the Indus River basin intensifies to serve two growing populations, Muslim-Hindu strife over falling water tables may be unavoidable.

"India and Pakistan will probably fall apart," Homer-Dixon predicts. "Their secular governments have less and less legitimacy as well as less management ability over people and resources." Rather than one bold line dividing the subcontinent into two parts, the future will likely see a lot of thinner lines and smaller parts, with the ethnic entities of Pakhtunistan and Punjab gradually replacing Pakistan in the space between the Central Asian plateau and the heart of the subcontinent.

None of this even takes into account climatic change, which, if it occurs in the next century, will further erode the capacity of existing states to cope. India, for instance, receives

70 percent of its precipitation from the monsoon cycle, which planetary warming could disrupt.

Not only will the three-dimensional aspects of the Last Map be in constant motion, but its two-dimensional base may change too. The National Academy of Sciences reports that

> as many as one billion people, or 20 per cent of the world's population, live on lands likely to be inundated or dramatically changed by rising waters. . . . Low-lying countries in the developing world such as Egypt and Bangladesh, where rivers are large and the deltas extensive and densely populated, will be hardest hit. . . . Where the rivers are dammed, as in the case of the Nile, the effects . . . will be especially severe.

Egypt could be where climatic upheaval—to say nothing of the more immediate threat of increasing population—will incite religious upheaval in truly biblical fashion. Natural catastrophes, such as the October 1992 Cairo earthquake, in which the government failed to deliver relief aid and slum residents were in many instances helped by their local mosques, can only strengthen the position of Islamic factions. In a statement about greenhouse warming which could refer to any of a variety of natural catastrophes, the environmental expert Jessica Tuchman Matthews warns that many of us underestimate the extent to which political systems, in affluent societies as well as in places like Egypt, "depend on the underpinning of natural systems." She adds, "The fact that one can move with ease from

Vermont to Miami has nothing to say about the consequences of Vermont acquiring Miami's climate."

Indeed, it is not clear that the United States will survive the next century in exactly its present form. Because America is a multiethnic society, the nation-state has always been more fragile here than it is in more homogeneous societies like Germany and Japan. James Kurth, in an article published in *The National Interest* in 1992, explains that whereas nation-state societies tend to be built around a mass-conscription army and a standardized public school system, "multicultural regimes" feature a high-tech, all-volunteer army (and, I would add, private schools that teach competing values), operating in a culture in which the international media and entertainment industry has more influence than the "national political class." In other words, a nation-state is a place where everyone has been educated along similar lines, where people take their cue from national leaders, and where everyone (every male, at least) has gone through the crucible of military service, making patriotism a simpler issue. Writing about his immigrant family in turn-of-the-century Chicago, Saul Bellow states, "The country took us over. It *was* a country then, not a collection of 'cultures.' "

During the Second World War and the decade following it, the United States reached its apogee as a classic nation-state. During the 1960s, as is now clear, America began a slow but unmistakable process of transformation. The signs hardly need belaboring: racial polarity, educational dysfunction, social fragmentation of many and various kinds. William Irwin Thompson, in *Passages About Earth: An Exploration of the New Planetary Culture*, writes, "The educational system that had worked on the Jews or the Irish could no longer work on the blacks; and when Jewish teachers in New York tried to take black children away from their parents exactly in the way they had been taken from theirs, they were shocked to encounter a violent affirmation of negritude."

Issues like West Africa could yet emerge as a new kind of foreign-policy issue, further eroding America's domestic peace. The spectacle of several West African nations collapsing at once could reinforce the worst racial stereotypes here at home. That is another reason why Africa matters. We must not kid ourselves: the sensitivity factor is higher than ever. The Washington, D.C., public school system is already experimenting with an Afrocentric curriculum. Summits between African leaders and prominent African-Americans are becoming frequent, as are Pollyanna-ish prognostications about multiparty elections in Africa that do not factor in crime, surging birth rates, and resource depletion. The Congressional Black Caucus was among those urging U.S. involvement in Somalia and in Haiti. At the *Los Angeles Times* minority staffers have protested against, among other things, what they allege to be the racist tone of the newspaper's Africa coverage, allegations that the editor of the "World Report" section, Dan Fisher, denies, saying essentially that Africa should be viewed through the same rigorous analytical lens as other parts of the world.

Africa may be marginal in terms of conventional late-twentieth-century conceptions of strategy, but in an age of cultural and racial clash, when national defense is increasingly local, Africa's distress will exert a destabilizing influence on the United States.

This and many other factors will make the United States less of a nation than it is today, even as it gains territory following the peaceful dissolution of Canada. Quebec, based on the bedrock of Roman Catholicism and Francophone ethnicity, could yet turn out to be North America's most cohesive and crime-free nation-state. (It may be a smaller Quebec, though, since aboriginal peoples may lop off northern parts of the province.) "Patriotism" will become increasingly regional as people in Alberta and Montana discover that they have far more in common with each other than they do with Ottawa or Washington, and Spanish-speakers in the Southwest discover a greater commonality with Mexico City. (*The Nine Nations of North America,* by Joel Garreau, a book about the continent's regionalization, is more relevant now than when it was published, in 1981.) As Washington's influence wanes, and with it the traditional symbols of American patriotism, North Americans will take psychological refuge in their insulated communities and cultures.

RETURNING FROM WEST AFRICA last fall was an illuminating ordeal. After leaving Abidjan, my Air Afrique flight landed in Dakar, Senegal, where all passengers had to disembark in order to go through another security check, this one demanded by U.S. authorities before they would permit the flight to set out for New York. Once we were in New York, despite the midnight hour, immigration officials at Kennedy Airport held up disembarkation by conducting quick interrogations of the aircraft's passengers—this was in addition to all the normal immigration and customs procedures. It was apparent that drug smuggling, disease, and other factors had contributed to the toughest security procedures I have ever encountered when returning from overseas.

Then, for the first time in over a month, I spotted businesspeople with attaché cases and laptop computers. When I had left New York for Abidjan, all the businesspeople were boarding planes for Seoul and Tokyo, which departed from gates near Air Afrique's. The only non-Africans off to West Africa had been relief workers in T-shirts and khakis. Although the borders within West Africa are increasingly unreal, those separating West Africa from the outside world are in various ways becoming more impenetrable.

But Afrocentrists are right in one respect: we ignore this dying region at our own risk. When the Berlin Wall was falling, in November 1989, I happened to be in Kosovo, covering a riot between Serbs and Albanians. The future was in Kosovo, I told myself that night, not in Berlin. The same day that Yitzhak Rabin and Yasser Arafat clasped hands on the White House lawn, my Air Afrique plane was approaching Bamako, Mali, revealing corrugated-zinc shacks at the edge of an expanding desert. The real news wasn't at the White House, I realized. It was right below.

II.

Was Democracy Just
a Moment?

(December 1997)

IN THE FOURTH CENTURY A.D. CHRISTIANITY'S CONQUEST of Europe and the Mediterranean world gave rise to the belief that a peaceful era in world politics was at hand, now that a consensus had formed around an ideology that stressed the sanctity of the individual. But Christianity was, of course, not static. It kept evolving, into rites, sects, and "heresies" that were in turn influenced by the geography and cultures of the places where it took root. Meanwhile, the church founded by Saint Peter became a ritualistic and hierarchical organization guilty of long periods of violence and bigotry. This is to say nothing of the evils perpetrated by the Orthodox churches in the East. Christianity made the world not more peaceful or, in practice, more moral but only more complex. Democracy, which is now overtaking the world as Christianity once did, may do the same.

The collapse of communism from internal stresses says nothing about the long-term viability of Western democracy. Marxism's natural death in Eastern Europe is no guarantee that subtler tyrannies do not await us, here and abroad. History has demonstrated that there is no final triumph of reason, whether it goes by the name of Christianity, the Enlightenment, or, now, democracy. To think that democracy as we know it will triumph—or is even here to stay—is itself a form of determinism, driven by our own ethnocentricity. Indeed, those who quote Alexis de Tocqueville in support of democracy's inevitability should pay heed to his observation that Americans, because of their (comparative) equality, exaggerate "the scope of human perfectibility." Despotism, Tocqueville went on, "is more particularly to be feared in democratic ages," because it thrives on the obsession with self and one's own security which equality fosters.

I submit that the democracy we are encouraging in many poor parts of the world is an integral part of a transformation toward new forms of authoritarianism; that democracy in the United States is at greater risk than ever before, and from obscure sources; and that many future regimes, ours especially, could resemble the oligarchies of ancient Athens and Sparta more than they do the current government in Washington. History teaches that it is exactly at such prosperous times as these that we need to maintain a sense of the tragic, however unnecessary it may seem. The Greek historian Polybius, of the second century B.C., interpreted what we consider the Golden Age of

Athens as the beginning of its decline. To Thucydides, the very security and satisfactory life that the Athenians enjoyed under Pericles blinded them to the bleak forces of human nature that were gradually to be their undoing in the Peloponnesian War.

My pessimism is, I hope, a foundation for prudence. America's Founders were often dismal about the human condition. James Madison: "Had every Athenian citizen been a Socrates, every Athenian assembly would still have been a mob." Thomas Paine: "Society is produced by our wants and government by our wickedness." It was the "crude" and "reactionary" philosophy of Thomas Hobbes, which placed security ahead of liberty in a system of enlightened despotism, from which the Founders drew philosophical sustenance. Paul A. Rahe, a professor of history at the University of Tulsa, shows in his superb three-volume *Republics Ancient and Modern* (1992) how the Founders partly rejected the ancient republics, which were based on virtue, for a utilitarian regime that channeled man's selfish, materialistic instincts toward benign ends. Man, Benjamin Franklin said in an apparent defense of Hobbesian determinism, is "a tool-making animal."

DEMOCRACIES ARE VALUE-NEUTRAL

HITLER AND MUSSOLINI each came to power through democracy. Democracies do not always make societies more civil—

but they do always mercilessly expose the health of the societies in which they operate.

In April 1985 I found myself in the middle of a Sudanese crowd that had just helped to overthrow a military regime and replace it with a new government, which the following year held free and fair elections. Sudan's newly elected democracy led immediately to anarchy, which in turn led to the most brutal tyranny in Sudan's postcolonial history: a military regime that broadened the scope of executions, persecuted women, starved non-Muslims to death, sold kidnapped non-Muslim children back to their parents for two hundred dollars, and made Khartoum the terrorism capital of the Arab world, replacing Beirut. In Sudan only 27 percent of the population (and only 12 percent of the women) could read. If a society is not in reasonable health, democracy can be not only risky but disastrous: during the last phases of the post–First World War German and Italian democracies, for example, the unemployment and inflation figures for Germany and the amount of civil unrest in Italy were just as abysmal as Sudan's literacy rates.

As an unemployed Tunisian student once told me, "In Tunisia we have a twenty-five percent unemployment rate. If you hold elections in such circumstances, the result will be a fundamentalist government and violence like in Algeria. First create an economy, then worry about elections." There are many differences between Tunisia and its neighbor Algeria, including the fact that Tunisia has been peaceful without democracy and Algeria erupted in violence in 1992 after its first election went awry and the military canceled the second. In Kurdistan and Afghanistan, two fragile tribal societies in which the United States encouraged versions of democracy in the 1990s, the security vacuums that followed the failed attempts at institutionalizing pluralism were filled by Saddam Hussein for a time in Kurdistan and by Islamic tyranny in much of Afghanistan. In Bosnia democracy legitimized the worst war crimes in Europe since the Nazi era. In sub-Saharan Africa democracy has weakened institutions and services in some states, and elections have been manipulated to restore dictatorship in others. In Sierra Leone and Congo-Brazzaville elections have led to chaos. In Mali, which Africa-watchers have christened a democratic success story, recent elections were boycotted by the opposition and were marred by killings and riots. Voter turnout was less than 20 percent. Even in Latin America, the Third World's most successful venue for democracy, the record is murky. Venezuela has enjoyed elected civilian governments since 1959, whereas for most of the 1970s and 1980s Chile was effectively under military rule. But Venezuela is a society in turmoil, with periodic coup attempts, rampant crime, and an elite that invests most of its savings outside the country; as a credit risk Venezuela ranks behind only Russia and Mexico. Chile has become a stable middle-class society whose economic growth rate compares to those of the Pacific Rim. Democratic Colombia is a pageant of bloodletting, and many members of the middle class are attempting to leave the country. Then there is Peru, where, all the faults of the present regime notwithstanding, a measure of stability has been achieved by a retreat from democracy into quasi-authoritarianism.

Throughout Latin America there is anxiety that unless the middle classes are enlarged and institutions modernized, the wave of democratization will not be consolidated. Even in an authentically democratic nation like Argentina, institutions are weak and both corruption and unemployment are high. President Carlos Menem's second term has raised questions about democracy's sustainability—questions that the success of his first term seemed to have laid to rest. In Brazil and other countries democracy faces a backlash from millions of badly educated and newly urbanized dwellers in teeming slums, who see few palpable benefits to Western parliamentary systems. Their discontent is a reason for the multifold increases in crime in many Latin American cities over the past decade.

Because both a middle class and civil institutions are required for successful democracy, democratic Russia, which inherited neither from the Soviet regime, remains violent, unstable, and miserably poor despite its 99 percent literacy rate. Under its authoritarian system China has dramatically improved the quality of life for hundreds of millions of its people. My point, hard as it may be for Americans to accept, is that Russia may be failing in part because it is a democracy and China may be succeeding in part because it is not. Having traveled through much of western China, where Muslim Turkic Uighurs (who despise the Chinese) often predominate, I find it hard to imagine a truly democratic China without at least a partial breakup of the country. Such a breakup would lead to chaos in western China, because the Uighurs are poorer and less educated than most Chinese and have a terrible historical record of governing themselves. Had the student demonstrations in 1989 in Tiananmen Square led to democracy, would the astoundingly high economic growth rates of the 1990s still obtain? I am not certain, because democracy in China would have ignited turmoil not just in the Muslim west of the country but elsewhere, too; order would have decreased but corruption would not have. The social and economic breakdown under democratic rule in Albania, where the tradition of precommunist bourgeois life is nonexistent (as in China), contrasted with more-successful democratic venues like Hungary and the Czech Republic, which have had well-established bourgeoisie, constitutes further proof that our belief in democracy regardless of local conditions amounts to cultural hubris.

Look at Haiti, a small country only ninety minutes by air from Miami, where twenty-two thousand American soldiers were dispatched in 1994 to restore "democracy." Five percent of eligible Haitian voters participated in an election last April, chronic instability continues, and famine threatens. Those who think that America can establish democracy the world over should heed the words of the late American theologian and political philosopher Reinhold Niebuhr:

The same strength which has extended our power beyond a continent has also . . . brought us into a vast web of history in which other wills, running in oblique or contrasting directions to our own, inevitably hinder or contradict what we most fervently desire. We cannot simply have our way, not even when we believe our way to have the "happiness of mankind" as its promise.

The lesson to draw is not that dictatorship is good and democracy bad but that democracy emerges successfully only as a capstone to other social and economic achievements. In his "Author's Introduction" to *Democracy in America,* Tocqueville showed how democracy evolved in the West not through the kind of moral fiat we are trying to impose throughout the world but as an organic outgrowth of development. European society had reached a level of complexity and sophistication at which the aristocracy, so as not to overburden itself, had to confer a measure of equality upon other citizens and allocate some responsibility to them: a structured division of the population into peacefully competing interest groups was necessary if both tyranny and anarchy were to be averted.

The very fact that we retreat to moral arguments—and often moral arguments only—to justify democracy indicates that for many parts of the world the historical and social arguments supporting democracy are just not there. Realism has come not from us but from, for example, Uganda's President Yoweri Museveni, an enlightened Hobbesian despot whose country has posted impressive annual economic growth rates —10 percent recently—despite tribal struggles in the country's north. In 1986 Museveni's army captured the Ugandan capital of Kampala without looting a single shop; Museveni postponed elections and saw that they took place in a manner that ensured his victory. "I happen to be one of those people who do not believe in multi-party democracy," Museveni has written. "In fact, I am totally opposed to it as far as Africa today is concerned. . . . If one forms a multi-party system in Uganda, a party cannot win elections unless it finds a way of dividing the ninety-four percent of the electorate [that consists of peasants], and this is where the main problem comes up: tribalism, religion, or regionalism becomes the basis for intense partisanship." In other words, in a society that has not reached the level of development Tocqueville described, a multiparty system merely hardens and institutionalizes established ethnic and regional divisions. Look at Armenia and Azerbaijan, where democratic processes brought nationalists to power upon the demise of the Soviet Union: each leader furthered his country's slide into war. A coup in Azerbaijan was necessary to restore peace and, by developing Azerbaijan's enormous oil resources, foster economic growth. Without the coup Western oil companies would not have gained their current foothold, which has allowed the United States to increase pressure on neighboring Iran at the same time that we attempt to normalize relations with Iran "on our terms."

Certainly, moral arguments in support of democracy were aired at the 1787 Constitutional Convention in Philadelphia, but they were tempered by the kind of historical and social analysis we now abjure. "The Constitution of the United States was written by fifty-five men—and one ghost," writes retired

Army Lieutenant General Dave R. Palmer in *1794: America, Its Army, and the Birth of the Nation* (1994). The ghost was that of Oliver Cromwell, the archetypal man on horseback who, in the course of defending Parliament against the monarchy in the mid–seventeenth century, devised a tyranny worse than any that had ever existed under the English Kings. The Founders were terrified of a badly educated populace that could be duped by a Cromwell, and of a system that could allow too much power to fall into one person's hands. That is why they constructed a system that filtered the whims of the masses through an elected body and dispersed power by dividing the government into three branches.

The ghosts of today we ignore—like the lesson offered by Rwanda, where the parliamentary system the West promoted was a factor in the murder of hundreds of thousands of Tutsis by Hutu militias. In 1992, responding partly to pressure from Western governments, the Rwandan regime established a multiparty system and transformed itself into a coalition government. The new political parties became masks for ethnic groups that organized murderous militias, and the coalition nature of the new government helped to prepare the context for the events that led to the genocide in 1994. Evil individuals were certainly responsible for the mass murder. But they operated within a fatally flawed system, which our own ethnocentric hubris helped to construct. Indeed, our often moralistic attempts to impose Western parliamentary systems on other countries are not dissimilar to the attempts of nineteenth-century Western colonialists—many of whom were equally idealistic—to replace well-functioning chieftaincy and tribal patronage systems with foreign administrative practices.

The demise of the Soviet Union was no reason for us to pressure Rwanda and other countries to form political parties—though that is what our post–Cold War foreign policy has been largely about, even in parts of the world that the Cold War barely touched. The Eastern European countries liberated in 1989 already had, in varying degrees, the historical and social preconditions for both democracy and advanced industrial life: bourgeois traditions, exposure to the Western Enlightenment, high literacy rates, low birth rates, and so on. The post–Cold War effort to bring democracy to those countries has been reasonable. What is less reasonable is to put a gun to the head of the peoples of the developing world and say, in effect, "Behave as if you had experienced the Western Enlightenment to the degree that Poland and the Czech Republic did. Behave as if ninety-five percent of your population were literate. Behave as if you had no bloody ethnic or regional disputes."

States have never been formed by elections. Geography, settlement patterns, the rise of literate bourgeoisie, and, tragically, ethnic cleansing have formed states. Greece, for instance, is a stable democracy partly because earlier in the century it carried out a relatively benign form of ethnic cleansing—in the form of refugee transfers—which created a monoethnic society. Nonetheless, it took several decades of economic development for Greece finally to put its coups behind it. Democracy often weakens states by necessitating ineffectual compromises and fragile coalition governments in societies where bureaucratic institutions never functioned well to begin with. Because democracy neither forms states nor strengthens them initially, multiparty systems are best suited to nations that already have efficient bureaucracies and a middle class that pays income tax, and where primary issues such as borders and power sharing have already been resolved, leaving politicians free to bicker about the budget and other secondary matters.

Social stability results from the establishment of a middle class. Not democracies but authoritarian systems, including monarchies, create middle classes—which, having achieved a certain size and self-confidence, revolt against the very dictators who generated their prosperity. This is the pattern today in the Pacific Rim and the southern cone of South America, but not in other parts of Latin America, southern Asia, or sub-Saharan Africa. A place like the Democratic Republic of Congo (formerly Zaire), where the per capita gross national product is less than two hundred dollars a year and the average person is either a rural peasant or an urban peasant; where there is little infrastructure of roads, sewers, and so on; and where reliable bureaucratic institutions are lacking, needs a leader like Bismarck or Jerry Rawlings—the Ghanaian ruler who stabilized his country through dictatorship and then had himself elected democratically—in place for years before he is safe from an undisciplined soldiery.

Foreign correspondents in sub-Saharan Africa who equate

democracy with progress miss this point, ignoring both history and centuries of political philosophy. They seem to think that the choice is between dictators and democrats. But for many places the only choice is between bad dictators and slightly better ones. To force elections on such places may give us some instant gratification. But after a few months or years a bunch of soldiers with grenades will get bored and greedy, and will easily topple their fledgling democracy. As likely as not, the democratic government will be composed of corrupt, bickering, ineffectual politicians whose weak rule never had an institutional base to start with: modern bureaucracies generally require high literacy rates over several generations. Even India, the great exception that proves the rule, has had a mixed record of success as a democracy, with Bihar and other poverty-wracked places remaining in semi-anarchy. Ross Munro, a noted Asia expert, has documented how Chinese autocracy has better prepared China's population for the economic rigors of the postindustrial age than Indian democracy has prepared India's.

Of course, our post–Cold War mission to spread democracy is partly a pose. In Egypt and Saudi Arabia, America's most important allies in the energy-rich Muslim world, our worst nightmare would be free and fair elections, as it would be elsewhere in the Middle East. The end of the Cold War has changed our attitude toward those authoritarian regimes that are not crucial to our interests—but not toward those that are. We praise democracy, and meanwhile we are grateful for an autocrat like King Hussein, and for the fact that the Turkish and

Pakistani militaries have always been the real powers behind the "democracies" in their countries. Obviously, democracy in the abstract encompasses undeniably good things such as civil society and a respect for human rights. But as a matter of public policy it has unfortunately come to focus on elections. What is in fact happening in many places requires a circuitous explanation.

THE NEW AUTHORITARIANISM

THE BATTLE BETWEEN liberal and neoconservative moralists who are concerned with human rights and tragic realists who are concerned with security, balance-of-power politics, and economic matters (famously, Henry Kissinger) is a variation of a classic dispute between two great English philosophers—the twentieth-century liberal humanist Isaiah Berlin and the seventeenth-century monarchist and translator of Thucydides, Thomas Hobbes.

In May 1953, while the ashes of the Nazi Holocaust were still smoldering and Stalin's grave was fresh, Isaiah Berlin delivered a spirited lecture against "historical inevitability"—the whole range of belief, advocated by Hobbes and others, according to which individuals and their societies are determined by their past, their civilization, and even their biology and environment. Berlin argued that adherence to historical inevitability, so disdainful of the very characteristics that make us human, led to Nazism and communism—both of them extreme attempts to force a direction onto history. Hobbes is just one of many famous philosophers Berlin castigated in his lecture, but it is Hobbes's bleak and elemental philosophy that most conveniently sums up what Berlin and other moralists so revile. Hobbes suggested that even if human beings are nobler than apes, they are nevertheless governed by biology and environment. According to Hobbes, our ability to reason is both a mask for and a slave to our passions, our religions arise purely from fear, and theories about our divinity must be subordinate to the reality of how we behave. Enlightened despotism is thus preferable to democracy: the masses require protection from themselves. Hobbes, who lived through the debacle of parliamentary rule under Cromwell, published his translation of Thucydides in order, he said, to demonstrate how democracy, among other factors, was responsible for Athens's decline. Reflecting on ancient Athens, the philosopher James Harrington, a contemporary and follower of Hobbes, remarked that he could think of "nothing more dangerous" than "debate in a crowd."

Though the swing toward democracy following the Cold War was a triumph for liberal philosophy, the pendulum will come to rest where it belongs—in the middle, between the ideals of Berlin and the realities of Hobbes. Where a political system leans too far in either direction, realignment or disaster awaits.

In 1993 Pakistan briefly enjoyed the most successful period of governance in its history. The government was neither de-

mocratic nor authoritarian but a cross between the two. The un-
elected Prime Minister, Moin Qureshi, was chosen by the President, who in turn was backed by the military. Because Qureshi
had no voters to please, he made bold moves that restored political stability and economic growth. Before Qureshi there had
been violence and instability under the elected governments of
Benazir Bhutto and Nawaz Sharif. Bhutto's government was essentially an ethnic-Sindhi mafia based in the south; Sharif's
was an ethnic-Punjabi mafia from the geographic center. When
Qureshi handed the country back to "the people," elections returned Bhutto to power, and chaos resumed. Finally, in November of last year, Pakistan's military-backed President again
deposed Bhutto. The sigh of relief throughout the country was
audible. Recent elections brought Sharif, the Punjabi, back to
power. He is governing better than the first time, but communal violence has returned to Pakistan's largest city, Karachi. I
believe that Pakistan must find its way back to a hybrid regime
like the one that worked so well in 1993; the other options are
democratic anarchy and military tyranny. (Anarchy and
tyranny, of course, are closely related: because power abhors a
vacuum, the one necessarily leads to the other. One day in 1996
Kabul, the Afghan capital, was ruled essentially by no one; the
next day it was ruled by Taliban, an austere religious movement.)

Turkey's situation is similar to Pakistan's. During the Cold
War, Turkey's military intervened when democracy threatened
mass violence, about once every decade. But Turkish coups are

no longer tolerated by the West, so Turkey's military has had to work behind the scenes to keep civilian governments from acting too irrationally for our comfort and that of many secular Turks. As elected governments in Turkey become increasingly circumscribed by the army, a quieter military paternalism is likely to evolve in place of periodic coups. The crucial element is not the name the system goes by but how the system actually works.

Peru offers another version of subtle authoritarianism. In 1990 Peruvian voters elected Alberto Fujimori to dismantle parts of their democracy. He did, and as a consequence he restored a measure of civil society to Peru. Fujimori disbanded Congress and took power increasingly into his own hands, using it to weaken the Shining Path guerrilla movement, reduce inflation from 7,500 percent to 10 percent, and bring investment and jobs back to Peru. In 1995 Fujimori won re-election with three times as many votes as his nearest challenger. Fujimori's use of deception and corporate-style cost-benefit analyses allowed him to finesse brilliantly the crisis caused by the terrorist seizure of the Japanese embassy in Lima. The commando raid that killed the terrorists probably never could have taken place amid the chaotic conditions of the preceding Peruvian government. Despite the many problems Fujimori has had and still has, it is hard to argue that Peru has not benefited from his rule.

In many of these countries Hobbesian realities—in particular, too many young, violence-prone males without jobs—

have necessitated radical action. In a York University study published last year the scholars Christian G. Mesquida and Neil I. Wiener demonstrate how countries with young populations (young poor males especially) are subject to political violence. With Third World populations growing dramatically (albeit at slowing rates) and becoming increasingly urbanized, democrats must be increasingly ingenious and dictators increasingly tyrannical in order to rule successfully. Surveillance, too, will become more important on an urbanized planet; it is worth noting that the etymology of the word "police" is *polis,* Greek for "city." Because tottering democracies and despotic militaries frighten away the investors required to create jobs for violence-prone youths, more hybrid regimes will perforce emerge. They will call themselves democracies, and we may go along with the lie—but, as in Peru, the regimes will be decisively autocratic. (Hobbes wrote that Thucydides "praiseth the government of Athens, when . . . it was democratical in name, but in effect monarchical under Pericles." Polybius, too, recommended mixed regimes as the only stable form of government.) Moreover, if a shortage of liquidity affects world capital markets by 2000, as Klaus Schwab, the president of the World Economic Forum, and other experts fear may happen, fiercer competition among developing nations for scarcer investment money will accelerate the need for efficient neo-authoritarian governments.

The current reality in Singapore and South Africa, for instance, shreds our democratic certainties. Lee Kuan Yew's offensive neo-authoritarianism, in which the state has evolved into a corporation that is paternalistic, meritocratic, and decidedly undemocratic, has forged prosperity from abject poverty. A survey of business executives and economists by the World Economic Forum ranked Singapore No. 1 among the fifty-three most advanced countries appearing on an index of global competitiveness. What is good for business executives is often good for the average citizen: per capital wealth in Singapore is nearly equal to that in Canada, the nation that ranks No. 1 in the world on the United Nations' Human Development Index. When Lee took over Singapore, more than thirty years ago, it was a mosquito-ridden bog filled with slum quarters that frequently lacked both plumbing and electricity. Doesn't liberation from filth and privation count as a human right? Jeffrey Sachs, a professor of international trade at Harvard, writes that "good government" means relative safety from corruption, from breach of contract, from property expropriation, and from bureaucratic inefficiency. Singapore's reputation in these regards is unsurpassed. If Singapore's 2.8 million citizens ever demand democracy, they will just prove the assertion that prosperous middle classes arise under authoritarian regimes before gaining the confidence to dislodge their benefactors. Singapore's success is frightening, yet it must be acknowledged.

Democratic South Africa, meanwhile, has become one of the most violent places on earth that are not war zones, according to the security firm Kroll Associates. The murder rate is six times that in the United States, five times that in Russia. There are ten private-security guards for every policeman. The currency has substantially declined, educated people continue to flee, and international drug cartels have made the country a new transshipment center. Real unemployment is about 33 percent, and is probably much higher among youths. Jobs cannot be created without the cooperation of foreign investors, but assuaging their fear could require the kind of union-busting and police actions that democracy will not permit. The South African military was the power behind the regime in the last decade of apartheid. And it is the military that may yet help to rule South Africa in the future. Like Pakistan but more so, South Africa is destined for a hybrid regime if it is to succeed. The abundant coverage of South Africa's impressive attempts at coming to terms with the crimes of apartheid serves to obscure the country's growing problems. There is a sense of fear in such celebratory, backward-looking coverage, as if writing too much about difficulties in that racially symbolic country would expose the limits of the liberal humanist enterprise worldwide.

Burma, too, may be destined for a hybrid regime, despite the deification of the opposition leader and Nobel Peace laureate Aung San Suu Kyi by Western journalists. While the United States calls for democracy in and economic sanctions against Burma, those with more immediate clout—that is, Burma's Asian neighbors, and especially corporate-oligarchic militaries like Thailand's—show no compunction about increasing trade links with Burma's junta. Aung San Suu Kyi may one day bear the title of leader of Burma, but only with the tacit approval of a co-governing military. Otherwise Burma will not be stable. A rule of thumb is that governments are determined not by what liberal humanists wish but rather by what businesspeople and others require. Various democratic revolutions failed in Europe in 1848 because what the intellectuals wanted was not what the emerging middle classes wanted. For quite a few parts of today's world, which have at best only the beginnings of a middle class, the Europe of the mid–nineteenth century provides a closer comparison than the Europe of the late twentieth century. In fact, for the poorest countries where we now recommend democracy, Cromwell's England may provide the best comparison.

As with the Christian religion (whose values are generally different for Americans than for Bosnian Serbs or for Lebanese Phalangists, to take only three examples), the nominal system of a government is less significant than the nature of the society in which it operates. And as democracy sinks into the soils of various local cultures, it often leaves less-than-nourishing deposits. "Democracy" in Cambodia, for instance, began evolving into something else almost immediately after the U.N.-sponsored elections there, in 1993. Hun Sen, one of two Prime Ministers in a fragile coalition, lived in a fortified bunker from which he physically threatened journalists and awarded government contracts in return for big bribes. His coup last summer, which toppled his co–Prime Minister and ended the democratic experiment, should have come as no surprise.

"World Government"

Authoritarian or hybrid regimes, no matter how illiberal, will still be treated as legitimate if they can provide security for their subjects and spark economic growth. And they will easily find acceptance in a world driven increasingly by financial markets that know no borders.

For years idealists have dreamed of a "world government." Well, a world government has been emerging—quietly and organically, the way vast developments in history take place. I do not refer to the United Nations, the power of which, almost by definition, affects only the poorest countries. After its peacekeeping failures in Bosnia and Somalia—and its $2 billion failure to make Cambodia democratic—the U.N. is on its way to becoming a supranational relief agency. Rather, I refer to the increasingly dense ganglia of international corporations and markets that are becoming the unseen arbiters of power in many countries. It is much more important nowadays for the leader of a developing country to get a hearing before corporate investors at the World Economic Forum than to speak before the U.N. General Assembly. Amnesty International now briefs corporations, just as it has always briefed national governments. Interpol officials have spoken about sharing certain kinds of intelligence with corporations. The Prime Minister of Malaysia, Mahathir Mohamad, is recognizing the real new world order (at least in this case) by building a low-tax district he calls a "multimedia super-corridor," with two new cities and a new air-port designed specifically for international corporations. The world's most efficient peacemaking force belongs not to the U.N. or even to the great powers but to a South African corporate mercenary force called Executive Outcomes, which restored relative stability to Sierra Leone in late 1995. (This is reminiscent of the British East India Company, which raised armies transparently for economic interests.) Not long after Executive Outcomes left Sierra Leone, where only 20.7 percent of adults can read, that country's so-called model democracy crumbled into military anarchy, as Sudan's model democracy had done in the late 1980s.

Of the world's hundred largest economies, fifty-one are not countries but corporations. While the two hundred largest corporations employ less than three-fourths of 1 percent of the world's work force, they account for 28 percent of world economic activity. The five hundred largest corporations account for 70 percent of world trade. Corporations are like the feudal domains that evolved into nation-states; they are nothing less than the vanguard of a new Darwinian organization of politics. Because they are in the forefront of real globalization while the overwhelming majority of the world's inhabitants are still rooted in local terrain, corporations will be free for a few decades to leave behind the social and environmental wreckage they create—abruptly closing a factory here in order to open an unsafe facility with a cheaper work force there. Ultimately, as technological innovations continue to accelerate and the world's middle classes come closer together, corporations may well become more responsible to the cohering global community and less amoral in the course of their evolution toward new political and cultural forms.

For instance, ABB Asea Brown Boveri Ltd. is a $36 billion-a-year multinational corporation divided into 1,300 companies in 140 countries; no one national group accounts for more than 20 percent of its employees. ABB's chief executive officer, Percy Barnevik, recently told an interviewer that this diversity is so that ABB can develop its own "global ABB culture—you might say an umbrella culture." Barnevik explains that his best managers are moved around periodically so that they and their families can develop "global personalities" by living and growing up in different countries. ABB management teams, moreover, are never composed of employees from any one country. Barnevik says that this encourages a "cross-cultural glue." Unlike the multiculturalism of the left, which masks individual deficiencies through collective—that is, ethnic or racial—self-esteem, a multinational corporation like ABB has created a diverse multicultural environment in which individuals rise or fall completely on their own merits. Like the hybrid regimes of the present and future, such an evolving corporate community can bear an eerie resemblance to the oligarchies of the ancient world. "Decentralization goes hand in hand with central monitoring," Barnevik says.

The level of social development required by democracy as it is known in the West has existed in only a minority of places—and even there only during certain periods of history. We are entering a troubling transition, and the irony is that while we preach our version of democracy abroad, it slips away from us at home.

THE SHRINKING DOMAIN OF "POLITICS"

I PUT SPECIAL emphasis on corporations because of the true nature of politics: who does and who doesn't have power. To categorize accurately the political system of a given society, one must define the significant elements of power within it. Supreme Court Justice Louis Brandeis knew this instinctively, which is why he railed against corporate monopolies. Of course, the influence that corporations wield over government and the economy is so vast and obvious that the point needs no elaboration. But there are other, more covert forms of emerging corporate power.

The number of residential communities with defended perimeters that have been built by corporations went from one thousand in the early 1960s to more than eighty thousand by the mid-1980s, with continued dramatic increases in the 1990s. ("Gated communities" are not an American invention. They are an import from Latin America, where deep social divisions in places like Rio de Janeiro and Mexico City make them necessary for the middle class.) Then there are malls, with their own rules and security forces, as opposed to public streets; private health clubs as opposed to public playgrounds; incorporated suburbs with strict zoning; and other mundane aspects of daily existence in which—perhaps without realizing it, because the changes have been so gradual—we opt out of the public sphere and the "social contract" for the sake of a protected setting. Dennis Judd, an urban-affairs expert at the University of Missouri at St. Louis, told me recently, "It's nonsense to think that Americans are individualists. Deep down we are a nation of herd animals: micelike conformists who will lay at our doorstep many of our rights if someone tells us that we won't have to worry about crime and our property values are secure. We have always put up with restrictions inside a corporation which we would never put up with in the public sphere. But what many do not realize is that life within some sort of corporation is what the future will increasingly be about."

Indeed, a number of American cities are re-emerging as Singapores, with corporate enclaves that are dedicated to global business and defended by private security firms adjacent to heavily zoned suburbs. For instance, in my travels I have looked for St. Louis and Atlanta and not found them. I found only hotels and corporate offices with generic architecture, "nostalgic" tourist bubbles, zoned suburbs, and bleak urban wastelands; there was nothing distinctive that I could label "St. Louis" or "Atlanta." Last year's Olympics in Atlanta will most likely be judged by future historians as the first of the postmodern era, because of the use of social façades to obscure fragmentation. Peace and racial harmony were continually proclaimed to be Olympic themes—even though whites and blacks in Atlanta live in separate enclaves and the downtown is a fortress of office blocks whose streets empty at dusk. During the games a virtual army was required to protect visitors from terrorism, as at previous Olympics, and also from random crime. All this seems normal. It is both wonderful and frightening how well we adapt.

Universities, too, are being redefined by corporations. I recently visited Omaha, where the corporate community made it possible for the Omaha branch of the University of Nebraska to build an engineering school—even after the Board of Regents vetoed the project. Local corporations, particularly First Data Resources, wanted the school, so they worked with the Omaha branch of the university to finance what became less a school than a large information-science and engineering complex. "This is the future," said the chancellor of the Omaha campus, Del Weber. "Universities will have to become entrepreneurs, working with corporations *on curriculum* [emphasis mine] and other matters, or they will die." The California state university system, in particular the San Diego campus, is perhaps the best example of corporate-academic synergy, in which a school rises in prestige because its curriculum has practical applications for nearby technology firms.

Corporations, which are anchored neither to nations nor to communities, have created strip malls, edge cities, and Disneyesque tourist bubbles. Developments are not necessarily bad: they provide low prices, convenience, efficient work forces, and, in the case of tourist bubbles, safety. We need big corporations. Our society has reached a level of social and technological complexity at which goods and services must be produced for a price and to a standard that smaller businesses cannot manage. We should also recognize, though, that the architectural reconfiguration of our cities and towns has been an undemocratic event—with decisions in effect handed down from above by an assembly of corporate experts.

"The government of man will be replaced by the administration of things," the Enlightenment French philosopher Henri de Saint-Simon prophesied. We should worry that experts will channel our very instincts and thereby control them to some extent. For example, while the government fights drug abuse, often with pathetic results, pharmaceutical corporations have worked *through* the government and political parties to receive sanction for drugs such as stimulants and antidepressants, whose consciousness-altering effects, it could be argued, are as great as those of outlawed drugs.

The more appliances that middle-class existence requires, the more influence their producers have over the texture of our lives. Of course, the computer in some ways enhances the power of the individual, but it also depletes our individuality. A degree of space and isolation is required for a healthy sense of self, which may be threatened by the constant stream of other people's opinions on computer networks.

Democratic governance, at the federal, state, and local levels, goes on. But its ability to affect our lives is limited. The growing piles of our material possessions make personal life more complex and leave less time for communal matters. And as communities become liberated from geography, as well as more specialized culturally and electronically, they will increasingly fall outside the realm of traditional governance. Democracy loses meaning if both rulers and ruled cease to be part of a community tied to a specific territory. In this historical transition phase, lasting perhaps a century or more, in which globalization has begun but is not complete and loyalties are highly confused, civil society will be harder to maintain. How and when we vote during the next hundred years may be a minor detail for historians.

True, there are strong similarities between now and a century ago. In the 1880s and 1890s America experienced great social and economic upheaval. The combination of industrialization and urbanization shook the roots of religious and family life: sects sprouted, racist Populists ranted, and single women, like Theodore Dreiser's Sister Carrie, went to work in filthy factories. Racial tensions hardened as the Jim Crow system took hold across the South. "Gadgets" like the light bulb and the automobile brought an array of new choices and stresses. "The city was so big, now, that people disappeared into it unnoticed," Booth Tarkington lamented in *The Magnificent Ambersons*.

A hundred years ago millionaires' mansions arose beside slums. The crass accumulation of wealth by a relatively small number of people gave the period its name—the Gilded Age, after a satire by Mark Twain and Charles Dudley Warner about financial and political malfeasance. Around the turn of the century 12 percent of all American households controlled about 86 percent of the country's wealth.

But there is a difference, and not just one of magnitude. The fortunes made from the 1870s through the 1890s by John D. Rockefeller, Andrew Carnegie, J. P. Morgan, and others were *American* fortunes, anchored to a specific geographic space. The Gilded Age millionaires financed an economy of scale to fit the vast landscape that Abraham Lincoln had secured by unifying the nation in the 1860s. These millionaires funded libraries and universities and founded symphony orchestras and historical societies to consolidate their own civilization in the making. Today's fortunes are being made in a global economic environment in which an affluent global civilization and power structure are being forged even as a large stratum of our society remains rooted in place. A few decades hence it may be hard to define an "American" city.

Even J. P. Morgan was limited by the borders of the nation-state. But in the future who, or what, will limit the likes of Disney chairman Michael Eisner? The U.N.? Eisner and those like him are not just representatives of the "free" market. Neither the Founders nor any of the early modern philosophers ever envisioned that the free market would lead to the concentration of power and resources that many corporate executives already embody. Whereas the liberal mistake is to think that there is a program or policy to alleviate every problem in the world, the conservative flaw is to be vigilant against concentrations of power in government only—not in the private sector, where power can be wielded more secretly and sometimes more dangerously.

UMPIRE REGIMES

THIS RISE OF CORPORATE POWER occurs more readily as the masses become more indifferent and the elite less accountable. Material possessions not only focus people toward private and away from communal life but also encourage docility. The more possessions one has, the more compromises one will make to protect them. The ancient Greeks said that the slave is someone who is intent on filling his belly, which can also mean someone who is intent on safeguarding his possessions. Aristophanes and Euripides, the late-eighteenth-century Scottish philosopher Adam Ferguson, and Tocqueville in the nineteenth century all warned that material prosperity would breed servility and withdrawal, turning people into, in Tocqueville's words, "industrious sheep."

In moderate doses, apathy is not necessarily harmful. I have lived and traveled in countries with both high voter turnouts and unstable politics; the low voter turnouts in the United States do not by themselves worry me. The philosopher James Harrington observed that the very indifference of most people allows for a calm and healthy political climate. Apathy, after all, often means that the political situation is healthy enough to be ignored. The last thing America needs is more voters—particularly badly educated and alienated ones—with a passion for politics. But when voter turnout decreases to around 50 percent at the same time that the middle class is spending astounding sums in gambling casinos and state lotteries, joining private health clubs, and using large amounts of stimulants and anti-depressants, one can legitimately be concerned about the state of American society.

I recently went to a basketball game at the University of Arizona. It was just a scrimmage, not even a varsity game. Yet the stadium was jammed, and three groups of cheerleaders performed. Season tickets were almost impossible to obtain, even before the team won the national championship. Donating $10,000 to $15,000 to the university puts one in a good position to accumulate enough points to be eligible for a season ticket, though someone could donate up to $100,000 and still not qualify. I have heard that which spouse gets to keep tickets can be a primary issue in Tucson divorce cases. I noticed that almost everyone in the stands was white; almost everyone playing was black. Gladiators in Rome were almost always of racial or ethnic groups different from the Romans. "There may be so little holding these southwestern communities together that a basketball team is all there is," a Tucson newspaper editor told me. "It's a sports team, a symphony orchestra, and a church rolled into one." Since neither Tucson nor any other southwestern city with a big state university can find enough talent locally, he pointed out, community self-esteem becomes a matter of which city can find the largest number of talented blacks from far away to represent it.

We have become voyeurs and escapists. Many of us don't play sports but love watching great athletes with great physical attributes. The fact that basketball and football and baseball have become big corporate business has only increased the popularity of spectator sports. Basketball in particular—so fluid, and with the players in revealing shorts and tank tops—provides the artificial excitement that mass existence "against instinct," as the philosopher Bertrand Russell labeled our lives, requires.

Take the new kind of professional fighting, called "extreme fighting," that has been drawing sellout crowds across the country. Combining boxing, karate, and wrestling, it has nothing fake about it—blood really flows. City and state courts have tried, often unsuccessfully, to stop it. The spectators interviewed in a CNN documentary on the new sport all appeared to be typical lower-middle- and middle-class people, many of whom brought young children to the fights. Asked why they came, they said that they wanted to "see blood." The mood of the Colosseum goes together with the age of the corporation, which offers entertainment in place of values. The Nobel laureate Czeslaw Milosz provides the definitive view on why Americans degrade themselves with mass culture: "Today man believes that there is *nothing* in him, so he accepts *anything*, even if he knows it to be bad, in order to find himself at one with others, in order not to be alone." Of course, it is because people find so little in themselves that they fill their world with celebrities. The masses avoid important national and international news because much of it is tragic, even as they show an unlimited appetite for the details of Princess Diana's death. This willingness to give up self and responsibility is the sine qua non for tyranny.

The classicist Sir Moses Finley ended his austere and penetrating work *Politics in the Ancient World* (1983) with these words:

> The ideology of a ruling class is of little use unless it is accepted by those who are being ruled, and so it was to an extraordinary degree in Rome. Then, when the ideology began to disintegrate within the elite itself, the consequence was not to broaden the political liberty among the citizenry but, on the contrary, to destroy it for everyone.

So what about our ruling class?

I was an expatriate for many years. Most expatriates I knew had utopian liberal beliefs that meant little, since few of them had much of a real stake in any nation. Their patriotism was purely nostalgic: a French friend would become tearful when her national anthem was played, but whenever she returned to France, she complained nonstop about the French. Increasingly, though, one can be an expatriate without living abroad. One can have Oriental rugs, foreign cuisines, eclectic tastes, exposure to foreign languages, friends overseas with whom one's life increasingly intertwines, and special schools for the kids—

all at home. Resident expatriatism, or something resembling it, could become the new secular religion of the upper-middle and upper classes, fostered by communications technology. Just as religion was replaced by nationalism at the end of the Middle Ages, at the end of modern times nationalism might gradually be replaced by a combination of traditional religion, spiritualism, patriotism directed toward the planet rather than a specific country, and assorted other organized emotions. Resident expatriates might constitute an elite with limited geographic loyalty beyond their local communities, which provide them with a convenient and aesthetically pleasing environment.

An elite with little loyalty to the state and a mass society fond of gladiator entertainments form a society in which corporate Leviathans rule and democracy is hollow. James Madison in *The Federalist* considered a comparable situation. Madison envisioned an enormously spread-out nation, but he never envisioned a modern network of transportation that would allow us psychologically to inhabit the same national community. Thus his vision of a future United States was that of a vast geographic space with governance but without patriotism, in which the state would be a mere "umpire," refereeing among competing interests. Regional, religious, and communal selfconcern would bring about overall stability. This concept went untested, because a cohesive American identity and culture did take root. But as Americans enter a global community, and as class and racial divisions solidify, Madison's concept is relevant anew.

There is something postmodern about this scenario, with its blend of hollow governance and fragmentation, and something ancient, too. Because of suburbanization, American communities will be increasingly segregated by race and class. The tendency both toward compromise and toward trusting institutions within a given community will be high, as in small and moderately sized European countries today, or as in ancient Greek city-states. Furthermore, prosperous suburban sprawls such as western St. Louis and western Omaha, and high-technology regions such as the Tucson-Phoenix corridor, North Carolina's Research Triangle, and the Portland-Seattle-Vancouver area will compete with one another and with individual cities and states for overseas markets, as North America becomes a more peaceful and productive version of chaotic, warring city-state Greece.

A continental regime must continue to function, because America's edge in information warfare requires it, both to maintain and to lead a far-flung empire of sorts, as the Athenians did during the Peloponnesian War. But trouble awaits us, if only because the "triumph" of democracy in the developing world will cause great upheavals before many places settle into more practical—and, it is to be hoped, benign—hybrid regimes. In the Middle East, for instance, countries like Syria, Iraq, and the Gulf sheikhdoms—with artificial borders, rising populations, and rising numbers of working-age youths—will not instantly become stable democracies once their absolute dictators and medieval ruling families pass from the scene. As in the early centuries of Christianity, there will be a mess.

Given the surging power of corporations, the gladiator culture of the masses, and the ability of the well-off to be partly disengaged from their own countries, what will democracy under an umpire regime be like?

THE RETURN OF OLIGARCHY?

SURPRISINGLY, THE FOUNDERS admired the military regime of Sparta. Only in this century has Sparta been seen as the forerunner of a totalitarian state. Why shouldn't men like Madison and George Washington have admired Sparta? Its division of power among two Kings, the elders, and the *ephors* ("overseers") approximated the system of checks and balances that the Founders desired in order to prevent the emergence of another Cromwell. Of course, Sparta, like Athens, was a two-tiered system, with an oligarchic element that debated and decided issues and a mass—*helots* ("serfs") in Sparta, and slaves and immigrants in Athens—that had few or no rights. Whether Sparta was a monarchy, an oligarchy, or a limited democracy—and whether Athens was oligarchic or democratic—still depends on one's viewpoint. According to Aristotle, "Whether the few or the many rule is accidental to oligarchy and democracy—the rich are few everywhere, the poor many." The real difference, he wrote, is that "oligarchy is to the advantage of the rich, democracy to the advantage of the poor." By "poor" Aristotle meant laborers, landowning peasants, artisans, and so on—essentially, the middle class and below.

Is it not conceivable that corporations will, like the rulers of both Sparta and Athens, project power to the advantage of the well-off while satisfying the twenty-first-century servile populace with the equivalent of bread and circuses? In other words, the category of politics we live with may depend more on power relationships and the demeanor of our society than on whether we continue to hold elections. Just as Cambodia was never really democratic, despite what the State Department and the U.N. told us, in the future we may not be democratic, despite what the government and media increasingly dominated by corporations tell us.

Indeed, the differences between oligarchy and democracy and between ancient democracy and our own could be far subtler than we think. Modern democracy exists within a thin band of social and economic conditions, which include flexible hierarchies that allow people to move up and down the ladder. Instead of clear-cut separations between classes there are many gray shades, with most people bunched in the middle. Democracy is a fraud in many poor countries outside this narrow band: Africans want a better life and instead have been given the right to vote. As new and intimidating forms of economic and social stratification appear in a world based increasingly on the ability to handle and analyze large quantities of information, a new politics might emerge for us, too—less like the kind envisioned by progressive reformers and more like the pragmatic hybrid regimes that are bringing prosperity to developing countries.

The classicist Sir Moses Finley has noted that what really separated the rulers from the ruled in the ancient world was literacy: the illiterate masses were subject to the elite's interpretation of documents. Analogous gulfs between rulers and ruled may soon emerge, not only because of differing abilities to process information and to master technology but also because of globalization itself. Already, barely literate Mexicans on the U.S. border, working in dangerous, Dickensian conditions to produce our VCRs, jeans, and toasters, earn less than fifty cents an hour, with no rights or benefits. Is that Western democracy or ancient-Greek-style oligarchy?

As the size of the U.S. population and the complexity of American life spill beyond the traditional national community, creating a new world of city-states and suburbs, the distance will grow between the citizens of the new city-states and the bureaucratic class of overseers in Washington. Those overseers will manage an elite volunteer military armed with information-age weapons, in a world made chaotic by the spread of democracy and its attendant neo-authoritarian heresies. We prevented the worst excesses of a "military-industrial complex" by openly fearing it, as President Dwight Eisenhower told us to do. It may be equally wise to fear a high-tech military complex today.

Precisely because the technological future in North America will provide so much market and individual freedom, this productive anarchy will require the supervision of tyrannies—or else there will be no justice for anyone. Liberty, after all, is inseparable from authority, as Henry Kissinger observed in *A World Restored: Metternich, Castlereagh and the Problems of Peace 1812–1822* (1957). A hybrid regime may await us all. The future of the Third World may finally be our own.

And that brings us to a sober realization. If democracy, the crowning political achievement of the West, is gradually being transfigured, in part because of technology, then the West will suffer the same fate as earlier civilizations. Just as Rome believed it was giving final expression to the republican ideal of the Greeks, and just as medieval Kings believed they were giving final expression to the Roman ideal, we believe, as the early Christians did, that we are bringing freedom and a better life to the rest of humankind. But as the nineteenth-century Russian liberal intellectual Alexander Herzen wrote, "Modern Western thought will pass into history and be incorporated in it . . . just as our body will pass into the composition of grass, of sheep, of cutlets, and of men." I do not mean to say that the United States is in decline. On the contrary, at the end of the twentieth century we are the very essence of creativity and dynamism. We are poised to transform ourselves into something perhaps quite different from what we imagine.

III.

IDEALISM WON'T STOP
MASS MURDER

(November 14, 1997)

AMERICAN FOREIGN POLICY THESE DAYS SEEMS IN-
creasingly grounded in a Holocaust mentality. Calls for the capture of Bosnian-Serb war criminals, for an impartial trial of
ex–Khmer Rouge leader Pol Pot, for justice in Rwanda, for the
establishment of an international war crimes tribunal, and the
especial fervor in which both liberals and neoconservatives now
defend human rights in places like China all have the Holocaust as a backdrop.

The conviction is gaining ground that mass murder, like
other deadly diseases, can be prevented by that remedy in
which all bourgeois societies, ours above all, deposit their faith,
Progress. In this case, progress in global public education: if
only Americans spread our values and the international community holds spectacular tribunals of war criminals, then genocide might become a thing of the past. Such an approach is

both noble and naive. Institutionalizing war-crimes tribunals will have as much effect on future war crimes as Geneva Conventions have had on the Iraqi and Serbian militaries.

MURDER BY ROTE

MASS MURDER IS a pathology of modernism, and particularly of highly centralized modern states, whether Mengistu Haile Mariam's Ethiopia, Pol Pot's "Democratic Kampuchea," or Hitler's Germany. Rwanda, a deceptively modern African nation, and Serb-held Bosnia, a warlord-cum-gangster enclave, fall into this category, too, because mass organization and bureaucratic orders were essential to the murder enterprise. In all these cases, the people who perform the killings inhabit a realm of experience so narrowly contained and brutal that they think and act almost by rote. They won't be influenced by outside pressure. The political leaders who preside over these killings may be, but here is where the issue of force against evil becomes confused.

The psychological and historical currents that ignite a bureaucratic killing machine often build for decades, even centuries. For example, the ideological abstractions of the Khmer Rouge were intensified by years of isolation in Southeast Asia's densest jungles prior to their takeover of Cambodia in 1975. The explosions of violence that follow are never inevitable. But if an outside power from thousands of miles away is to halt such a process suddenly in its tracks it must be serious about it—serious enough to use deadly force.

Moral interventionists argue that genocide in and of itself constitutes a strategic risk to America, since if anything goes then world order is further undermined. But that logic conveniently ignores what the American public has historically required for an event to qualify as a threat to the national interest, and thus merit troops. Callously put, the murder of up to a million Tutsis in Rwanda did not affect the United States. Somalia reminded us of this eternal truth of American overseas involvements: human suffering may sometimes be sufficient to get U.S. troops flown to a place, but the moment they start taking casualties there better be a specific national interest at stake, and one that can be communicated succinctly on television, or else the public will cut and run. Haiti did not test that truth. Bosnia hasn't yet.

Only when moral interests crosshatch with strategic ones will the public tolerate blood in an intervention. Hitler's war against the Jews did not get us into World War II—the attack on Pearl Harbor did. Saddam's gassing of the Kurds did not lead to U.S. intervention; his threat to Saudi oil fields did. Bosnian war crimes did not, by themselves, lead to NATO intervention: it was also the larger Balkan war and the fear of it spreading south, and the threat posed by all of these factors to NATO's credibility, that finally forced President Clinton's hand.

Another problem is that war criminals are most vulnerable to capture when their political power is spent, or at least on the wane (as Radovan Karadzic's is). Until then, someone will often have a use for them. In the 1980s, we supported the Khmer Rouge as a wedge against the Soviet Union after they had murdered over a million people, a policy that while despicable was not irrational given the Cold War. Sometimes war criminals need to be helped, as when U.S. policy makers armed Croatian troops, in order to restore the regional balance of power. This advanced, in turn, the Dayton Peace Accords. Sometimes Realpolitik demands that war criminals be pardoned—as when hordes of guilty, lower-level Germans were amnestied after World War II to hasten the rebuilding of West Germany, because of the Soviet threat. Justice will prove more elusive than we think.

Another problem (and irony) is that some cherished Western ideals—democracy, freedom, self-determination—sometimes lead to wholesale murder when coupled with ethnic hatreds. The Jews of Baghdad who survived an Arab pogrom in 1941 certainly did not look forward to the end of British colonialism, or for that matter, any freedom or democratization whatsoever for the Arab masses. Likewise, ethnic minorities in the Balkans rightly feared the end of Austro-Hungarian and Ottoman rule. The late Baghdadi Jew Elie Kedourie wrote that in "the right of conquest," by the British or anyone else, the Jews "could cheerfully acknowledge, for all their history had taught them that there lay safety."

Alas, protection against evil is surest when man is assumed to be wholly unimprovable. That is a dilemma that liberal internationalism, which subscribes to Progress, has never satisfactorily dealt with. The policy that best incorporates such a bleak view of humanity is "balance of power"—or, more precisely, balance-of-fear-and-intimidation. Because this is neither a new nor an interesting nor an inspiring idea, it is easily relegated when debate focuses on high-minded pursuits like preventing mass murder. But the balance of power is the sine qua non without which warding off genocide becomes impossible.

STALINIST NIGHTMARE

IT WAS NOT just the failure to contain Nazi Germany continentally and Serbia regionally that prove this, but in a more precise way, Ethiopia in 1977 and 1978. There, President Carter's well-intentioned human rights policy became a barrier to the sort of action necessary to save over thirty million people from the fist of totalitarianism. While Mr. Carter refused to deal at all with the Mengistu regime because of its gross human rights violations, the Soviets sent East German security experts to Addis Ababa to help Mengistu consolidate his rule. Because we stood on principle and were, therefore, absent as any kind of a countervailing force, it wasn't just another awful and vicious regime that emerged, but a Stalinist nightmare. Millions were brutally collectivized, and millions more died of famine.

The Cold War is over, but dealing with bad people will always be necessary to prevent even greater evil. Pessimism can be a more efficient line of defense against genocide than any human rights policy—as many Israelis, for example, intuitively grasp.

For Israel, after all, is the only nation in history whose state system directly incorporates the lessons of mass murder. And what are those lessons? The need for an advantageous balance of power in the region, and a powerful military, but also for lethal security services that both provide early warning and instill fear of the kind civil societies do not tolerate. In fact, the very intelligence services that we often denigrate and, in some cases, want to dismantle would be precisely what we need to warn us in advance of the threat of genocide.

Remember that for Israeli policy makers, war-crimes trials are a weapon held in check for rare occasions only. When they're used, it is as an accessory to the daily actions of the country's military-security machine. And when Israelis say Never Again, they mean never again to Jews: other people will have to take care of themselves.

But many Americans think that it may be possible to afford some protection to all those other people. If so, I fear that we may have to be very ruthless indeed.

IV.

SPECIAL INTELLIGENCE

(February 1998)

THE UNITED STATES MILITARY, FOR ALL ITS SEX SCAN-dals, has an easy time with the media in comparison with the Central Intelligence Agency. Media criticism of the military is periodically mixed with awe, as when journalists reported the successes of the Gulf War, made heroes out of Generals Colin Powell and Norman Schwarzkopf, and lionized bridge-construction units in Bosnia. But media criticism of the CIA is so constant and blistering that it suggests a hatred of the intelligence profession itself—or at least a feeling that spy agencies are obsolete in a post–Cold War information age. That is ironic, because the intelligence industry is sure to become even more necessary for our well-being, and therefore more powerful within government.

That was one conclusion I reached after serving briefly as a consultant to the Army's Special Forces Regiment at Fort

Bragg, North Carolina. Special Forces are a military growth industry. The new chairman of the Joint Chiefs of Staff, General Henry H. Shelton, comes from the Special Operations Forces. In 1996 U.S. Special Forces were responsible for 2,325 missions in 167 countries involving 20,642 people—only nine per operation, on average. Words like "low-key" and "discreet" are frequently used by Special Forces members to describe what they do. Considering that the threat posed by Russian mafias and Russian nuclear terrorists is now greater than that posed by Russian tanks and infantry, the military usefulness of the North Atlantic Treaty Organization will depend more on the integration of Special Forces within NATO's largely conventional command than on the integration of the Czech Republic and other former Eastern-bloc states. Then there are the gas and oil pipelines soon to be built through unstable tribal lands around the Caspian Sea, which will need protection; mounting problems with drug cartels; a predicted upsurge in the kidnapping of rich and politically prominent people and their children; the increase in climatic catastrophe, now that human beings are inhabiting flood- and earthquake-prone regions to an unprecedented extent; and worldwide rapid-fire urbanization. All these augment the importance of lean and mobile military units that conflate the traditional categories of police officers, commandos, emergency-relief specialists, diplomats, and, of course, intelligence officers.

The public will demand protection—for as few tax dollars as possible—from a whole new kind of enemy that is using technology to miniaturize and conceal explosives and communications devices. The future will thus be brutal to industrial-age armies with big tanks and jets, and kind to corporate-style forces in urban settings, which rely on both electronic and human intelligence. In recent years various spy agencies provided information that led to the capture of plutonium smugglers. In contrast, the extensive use of conventional troops to change the regime in Haiti was both costly and unpopular—despite the lack of bloodshed. The old, pre-Vietnam method for Haiti would have been to use both the intelligence service and Special Forces to ease out or topple a cruel and incompetent regime. That method might have avoided the challenge of instituting democracy, but it would have been quieter and less time-consuming—and cheaper. Although we won't often topple regimes in the future, the urge will grow to use what the Army calls "quiet professionals" to neutralize problems that the public does not consider to be of urgent national interest. An urban geographer with whom I recently spoke told me that Vancouver—a typical emerging city-state with a productive economy and its own strategic transport links—will have no particular need for either Canada or the United States. But it will require a protective shield of the kind that Washington's Special Forces and intelligence units can provide.

SPECIAL FORCES ACTIVITIES range from backpacking around the Thai-Burmese border in a quest for information about drug smuggling to conducting surveillance for the Bosnian peace-keeping operation. Along with the usual commando skills and an emphasis on urban fighting, the subjects taught at the John F. Kennedy Special Warfare Center and School at Fort Bragg include dentistry, ophthalmology, veterinary medicine, X-ray interpretation, well-digging, negotiating, and exotic languages. The aim is to create a force of men (women are not yet eligible for Special Forces) that can (this time) truly win "hearts and minds," by acting as doctors and aid workers in a Third World city or village—and also, if need be, can kill or apprehend a war criminal, a terrorist group, or another adversary. At a recent Special Forces conference I observed an auditorium full of 1990s commandos who looked markedly different from the Vietnam-era warriors who occupied the first two rows as honored guests. The Vietnam-era men, most of them in their fifties, looked thuggish: guys without necks and occasionally with tattoos, guys you would not want to meet in the dark. The rest of the auditorium resembled a group of graduate students who happened to be in excellent physical shape.

The conflation of roles is not something new and futuristic but something old and traditional. The Army is essentially re-creating colonial expeditionary forces with men who are chameleons, modeled after the spy, linguist, and master of disguise Sir Richard Francis Burton. "Ambiguity," "subjective" and "intuitive" thinking, and decisions made when only 20 percent of the evidence is in are encouraged: by the time more information is available, it will be too late to act. Nor are cultural generalizations about what Fort Bragg instructors call "modal personalities" frowned on. For instance, I sat in on a class in which the instructor, an Arabic-speaker who had lived for years in the Middle East, said that because of the authoritarian nature of Arab militaries, Arab noncommissioned officers don't make decisions on their own. He added that rote learning and an emphasis on memory mean that Arab pilots do not always use manuals for preflight checks, as U.S. pilots do.

That is stereotyping. But commandos don't have the luxury of exploring individuals. A certain amount of generalization is needed to predict how potentially hostile forces may behave. The assumption at Fort Bragg is that despite war-crimes tribunals and Geneva Conventions, future adversaries will play by the rules even less often than present ones do. Terrorism, drug smuggling, money laundering, industrial espionage, and so on will all evolve into new forms of "conventional" warfare that provide authoritarian leaders with the means to wage war without ever acknowledging it.

For an army that will have to act secretly, unconventionally, and in advance of crises rather than during them, intelligence is critical. Indeed, the growth of Special Forces might be a crude indication of the collapse of any distinction between our military and intelligence services. Yes, the CIA itself might be done away with. What the CIA does, however, will not only grow in importance but also have the support of armed troops within the same bureaucratic framework.

Pakistan's Inter-Services Intelligence Agency is akin to the CIA—except that it has essentially its own private army. While Pakistan has grown weaker as a state, with near anarchy prevailing in Karachi, its regional power has grown, thanks to the ISI. The Taliban religious movement in Afghanistan, for instance, in its recent sudden rise received help from the ISI, which wanted to resurrect trade routes through Afghanistan to Iran. This kind of influence may sound frightening, but it is efficient compared with what we have now.

Ever since the ancient soothsayers of the Delphic oracle there have been intelligence agencies of one sort or another. Spying is as old as war itself. Moses sent spies into Canaan. An important factor that led to Pearl Harbor was a lack of enough good intelligence: The CIA, in its current form, may eventually pass out of existence, but in a world in which borders are dissolving and bad guys conceal bombs in their pockets or steal millions by means of computers, the intelligence business is set for a golden age.

V.

AND NOW FOR THE NEWS:
THE DISTURBING FRESHNESS
OF GIBBON'S *DECLINE AND FALL*

(March 1997)

RECENTLY, IN THE COURSE OF PACKING BOOKS AWAY for storage, I came across an old friend—Edward Gibbon's *The History of the Decline and Fall of the Roman Empire*. I decided to hold out three of the six volumes for yet another reading. As when I had read the *Decline and Fall* previously, I was deliciously overwhelmed. If I could have one voice in my ear as I traveled through the Third World, with its innumerable rebellions and migrations; through Europe, as nationalism impedes unification; or through the United States, as it tries to reconstitute itself for a transnational age, the voice would be Gibbon's, with its sly wit, biting irony, and fearless realism about an event that "is still felt by the nations of the earth." The collapse of Rome left in its wake the tribal configurations from which modern European states emerged, and I can think of no work that offers a shrewder historical perspective on today's foreign and domestic news than the three volumes of the *Decline and Fall* that cover Rome from its territorial zenith, in the early second century A.D., under Trajan (the first and last Roman general to navigate the Persian Gulf), to the dissolution of the western half of the empire, in A.D. 476.

Those three volumes, published from 1776 to 1781—the years of the American Revolution—offer, of course, more than the story of Rome's decline. Among other things, they constitute a general theory of history, a controversial interpretation of the birth of Christianity, an extended essay on military elites and the fickleness of public opinion, and an unequaled geographical and cultural primer on Europe, the Middle East, and Asia. Beyond all else, though, the *Decline and Fall* is a page-turning narrative, driven by the most pointed of character sketches and anecdotes, without which, regardless of its other strengths, Gibbon's work would never have survived. Of the younger Gordion, who ruled Rome for little more than a month in A.D. 237, Gibbon wrote: "Twenty-two acknowledged concubines, and a library of sixty-two thousand volumes, attested the variety of his inclinations, and from the productions which he left behind him, it appears that the former as well as the latter were designed for use rather than ostentation." Following that is a footnote, in which Gibbon added, "By each of his concubines, the younger Gordion left three or four children. His literary productions were by no means contemptible."

Gibbon's Rome from the second through the fifth centuries offers a rich and riveting tableau of coups, countercoups, wicked savagery, ethnic and regional upheavals, and attempts at reform that either failed or, sometimes worse, succeeded, the success creating new problems that furthered Rome's decline—as though an empire (or any large state) were a living organism "subject to decay," as Polybius would have it, from "its own internal evolution," good or bad.

The *Decline and Fall* instructs that human nature never changes, and that mankind's predilection for faction, augmented by environmental and cultural differences, is what determines history. In this Gibbon was influenced by the Baron de Montesquieu, who saw history not as mere politics and ideas but as a complex of cultural, social, and climatic forces. The brilliance of the *Decline and Fall* lies in Gibbon's ability to build a narrative out of individual agency and the surprises of history—such as the empire's restoration in the third century under the able rule of Claudius, Aurelian, Probus, and Diocletian—even as the sheer accumulation and repetition of events over centuries ultimately robs many an effective emperor (each with a distinct personality early in the story) of his identity in the reader's mind. And as the initially successful restoration flows into the larger movement of decline, only patterns, rather than individuals, endure at the end of the three volumes.

For Gibbon the real changes were not so much the dramatic, "newsworthy" events as the insidious transformations: Rome moving from democracy to the trappings of democracy to military rule; Milan in Italy and Nicomedia in Asia Minor functioning as capital cities decades before the formal division of the empire into western and eastern halves, and almost two centuries before Rome officially ceased to be an imperial capital; the fact that the first fifteen "Christian" bishops of Jerusalem were circumcised Jews subscribing to a not yet formalized religion. It seems that the more gradual and hidden the change, the more historically important it turned out to be.

THE SIMILARITIES BETWEEN Gibbon's Rome and the United States will be obvious to any reader—they are two multiethnic polities founded on patriotic virtue, unified by gigantic highway systems, their middle classes occupying crassly uniform dwellings, and so forth—but the *Decline and Fall* evokes other contemporary realities. Gibbon's catalog of ancient authoritarian regimes also depicts places like Nigeria, Pakistan, Serbia, Nicolae Ceaușescu's Romania, and mid-twentieth-century Germany, Japan, and the Soviet Union—without, of course, the mass organization and mass murder allowed for by industrialization. It was the peripatetic Emperor Caracalla, in the early third century, Gibbon tells us—not Hitler or Stalin or even Attila the Hun—who was the first worldwide tyrant. And when Gibbon wrote about the Crimean Chersonites, who, helped by the Romans, attacked the Goths in A.D. 335, he captured well the nearby Caucasus, where the Russians now pit one assemblage of clans against another. The *Decline and Fall* teaches that the tragedy for so much of the world is how, despite technological advancement, various societies are still in a political sense ancient; and how, despite the Enlightenment, many governments—including ours—remain corrupt and decadent because of the influence of money.

Gibbon's writing sets a standard for literary bravery. He sought no one's approval and was afraid of nothing. In his day the Church was a sacred cow; he was merciless in his exposition of its evolution. According to Gibbon, Christianity—to use the words of the historian Hugh Trevor-Roper in his introduction to the *Decline and Fall*—emerged from a "heretical Jewish sect" to become a "novel cult of virginity" and the most "persistent of the competing new Oriental superstitions," eventually to capture power as a "revolutionary ideology." Concerning the persecutions of the Christians, Gibbon concluded, after exhaustive documentation,

> Even admitting, without hesitation or inquiry, all that history has recorded, or devotion has feigned, on the subject of martyrdoms, it must still be acknowledged that the Christians, in the course of their intestine dissensions, have inflicted far greater severities on each other than they had experienced from the zeal of infidels.

Not surprisingly, the publication of the *Decline and Fall* met with bitter controversy. Though the book was praised by the philosopher David Hume and others, attacks on Gibbon for his treatment of the Church were widespread and sustained: almost sixty denunciatory books about him were published in his lifetime. Bad reviews forced Gibbon to write a vindication of his first volume in 1779; he did it brilliantly. Attempts to undermine the *Decline and Fall* continued.

Rather than the embodiment of amoral despair, Gibbon revealed himself as the very flower of Enlightenment rationalism. He was a conservative along the lines of his contemporary Edmund Burke, who saw humankind's best hope in moderate politics and elastic institutions that do not become overbearing. Only rarely did imperial Rome or early Christianity display the necessary traits. Gibbon, like Burke, was shocked by the French Revolution. His Rome had also known violent mobs screaming noble platitudes in order to remove a tyrannical ruler, only to see another one set in his place. Gibbon's certainty that the tendency toward strife is a natural consequence of the human condition—a natural consequence of the very variety of our racial, cultural, and economic experience, which no belief system, religious or otherwise, can overcome—is reminiscent of James Madison in *The Federalist*. Madison, too, was convinced that a state or an empire can endure only if it generally limits itself to adjudicating disputes among its peoples, and in so doing becomes an exemplar of patriotic virtue.

To dip into the *Decline and Fall* is to know what not only writing but also reading used to be like. Gibbon's elliptical elegance is rare in an age when a surfeit of information, coupled with the distractions of electronic communication, forces writers to move briskly from one point to another. Rare, too, in an age of tedious academic specialty are Gibbon's sweeping yet valuable generalizations. When Gibbon describes everyday people in poor nations as exhibiting a "carelessness of futurity," he exposes one tragic effect of underdevelopment in a way that many more-careful and polite tomes of today do not. Our academic clerisy, I'm sure, could point out factual inadequacies, along with examples of cultural bias, throughout the *Decline and Fall.* Yet nothing on the shelves today will give readers as awe-inspiring a sense of spectacle as the *Decline and Fall:* of how onrushing events almost everywhere—Europe, Africa, the Near East, Asia—so seamlessly weave together. At a time of sound bites on one hand and five-hundred-page yawns about a single issue on the other, here, blessedly, is something for the general reader.

VI.

PROPORTIONALISM: A REALISTIC APPROACH TO FOREIGN POLICY

(August 1996)

We are all wringing our hands over the plight of failing, unstable regions of the Third World, especially those in sub-Saharan Africa. But there is little consensus on what the American response should be. Many liberals blame the West and racism for the Third World's ills, and believe that democracy and foreign-aid programs can defeat historical, cultural, and environmental forces that have been at work for centuries. Some conservatives think that the free market is the answer to everyone's problems; other conservatives think that even a display of interest in a place like Africa indicates naïve do-goodism. At one extreme is Pat Buchanan, at the Mexican border with a gun and a black cowboy hat, holding off the tide of darker peoples. At the other extreme is Mrs. Jellyby, in Dickens's *Bleak House*, whose eyes "could see nothing nearer than Africa!" Mrs. Jellyby let her London household go to ruin while she wrote letters all day in support of a tribe on the Niger River. Caught among the various mind-sets are well-meaning Washington bureaucrats who are trying to craft workable policies on global humanitarian issues.

A durable foreign-aid consensus—one that might do gradual but unmistakable good where good can in fact be done— must be built on two seemingly contrary realizations:

- Although some human societies have made end runs around their own histories and environments, exceptionalism is, well, the exception. The fact that Africa continues to fall economically behind the Indian subcontinent (the second poorest region on the planet), despite billions spent on development assistance over the decades, amounts to an inescapable negative judgment. Not even Russia, with its 150 million people, 99 percent of whom are literate, can be pivotally affected by aid. To think that aid can fundamentally change sub-Saharan Africa, whose population is 3.75 times that of Russia and whose literacy rate is much, much lower, is to take a position that few people outside a narrow intellectual elite will accept. It is not even clear that American exceptionalism can be counted on: we will have less money in the future for foreign aid, not more.

- Although development assistance rarely changes history dramatically, it can do significant good in a significant number of places. And it can do good in ways that help us to reinvent ourselves as a nation in the context of a more interconnected world, while also promoting vital security interests. A growing African middle class, for instance, would constitute an enormous market for American products. An Africa in which viruses could be monitored and controlled would preserve AIDS as a singularity rather than a harbinger of more pandemics. Given that disease is affected by poverty, migration, and environmental trends, helping Africa is strategically important if only in terms of cold self-interest.

A DEVELOPMENT POLICY toward the underdeveloped world must have the ability to win political support in Washington and the nation at large. This is a simple fact that no amount of idealism or wishful thinking can get around. A development policy must engage us without overstraining us. Its criteria must be clear. And it must not set us up for failure. Expensive stunts like the invasions of Somalia and Haiti are risky in the context of an isolationist-tending climate of political discourse. If such endeavors fail, they threaten funding for useful programs in politically and economically fragile places where hope survives.

Herein is a rough sketch for a Third World aid policy. It is inspired in some measure by the principle known as proportionalism, adopted by some Catholic theologians on certain vexing moral issues. Proportionalism provides a useful moral approach to the Third World. In theological terms proportionalism is about doing or accepting a certain amount of "evil" to make possible a proportionately greater amount of good; it underlies theories of a just war and also, for some Catholics, the argument in favor of promoting the use of contraceptives as a means of reducing abortion. In everyday, nontheological terms it is about beating a retreat in order to preserve what is most important. Proportionalism is anathema to moral and ideological purists. It tempers implacable principle with common sense.

Foreign-aid proportionalism would have three aspects: the aid itself, early warning, and extremely rare interventions. What follows is a framework for disparate ideas and policies that have been bruited about and in some cases partly implemented.

First, the foreign aid itself would not be increased overall, because forging a political consensus for maintaining levels as they are is hard enough. But it would be targeted at bread-and-butter regionwide programs that seek to slow societal deterioration gradually, in order to create an environment for the emergence of healthier politics. It would *not* be targeted at making a particular country democratic in the face of a low literacy rate, the absence of a middle class, and a history of ethnic or regional strife. The Washington establishment chants that democracies don't go to war, but what are emerging in many places are pseudodemocracies, societies teetering on ungovernability which hold elections out of desperation rather than as the final step in a process of economic and political development. Reduced emphasis on "democratic elections" would mean a new emphasis instead on population control, women's literacy, and resource-renewal projects. If more conservatives knew, for example, that an 85 percent cut in U.S. Agency for International Development family-planning programs would lead to 1.6 million more abortions a year by desperate women in developing countries, enough of them might support renewing these programs to form a majority with liberals. Moreover, it has been shown that increased literacy among women reduces the birth rate: literate women exert more power in their relationships with men, control their own lives and those of their children better, and use financial and natural resources more intelligently. Nothing promotes positive social evolution in the Third World more speedily than women's education.

Second, early warning. Some equate pessimism about the Third World with cynicism. In truth, pessimism is often both a realistic and a moral response: we *should* be scouting for trouble, not indulging fond hope. Probing for trouble in advance—as the United States is doing now in Burundi—will not always pay dividends. But there will be times when conflict management sooner will forestall more agonizing choices later.

The third aspect is intervention—the rarer the better. The so-called Powell Doctrine—which calls for intervention only when it can be quickly and easily accomplished—has been criticized for moral obtuseness. But the Powell Doctrine is in fact a good start. The degree of difficulty of a humanitarian relief operation *must* be a criterion in making a decision, for if it is not, our misadventures will preclude intervention even when intervention would otherwise have been worthwhile. The other criteria should be the strategic value of the place where we are considering intervening and the psychological weight that such an intervention might exert on other parts of the world. Interventions in places and situations in which morality coincides with ease, strategic value, and leverage would meet what the military calls the parents' test: when a Pentagon official can stare a soldier's parents in the eye and tell them that their son or daughter died in the service of something worth dying for. (There are situations in which the strategic value is significant but so is the difficulty—such as in the Balkans and on the Korean peninsula. These places are historical legacies of sacrifices in three wars that saw great losses of American lives, and compared with which our historical involvement in a place like Liberia pales in significance.) In any case, here is George F. Kennan, cautioning against intervention in Somalia—a warning that applies to other Third World states that have gone into the abyss.

> The fact is that this dreadful situation cannot possibly be put to rights other than by the establishment of a governing power for the entire territory, and a very ruthless, determined one at that. It would not be a democratic one, because the very pre-requisites for a democratic political system do not exist among the people in question.

The framework outlined above accepts a certain amount of evil (diminished concern for elections; a willingness in many cases to stand by and watch atrocious situations without intervening) in order to pursue an attainable good (low-risk, high-yield interventions only, and only on rare occasions; modest but clear involvement in literacy and other bread-and-butter programs in places where improvement is possible). We must stay engaged, but within strict limits.

VII.

KISSINGER, METTERNICH, AND REALISM

(June 1999)

TIME CHANGES REPUTATIONS. THE CURRENT FAVORABLE reconsideration of Henry Kissinger may have less to do with the recent publication of his final volume of memoirs than with the lackluster quality of his successors at the State Department. Cyrus Vance, Edmund Muskie, Alexander Haig, Lawrence Eagleburger, and Warren Christopher are footnotes to history. George Shultz and James Baker were more substantial presences, but their substance had much more to do with their common sense than with their intellectual creativity (of which Shultz had some and Baker less). Then there is Madeleine Albright, who was hailed at first as having the perfect combination of gutsiness, idealism, and policy savvy, but who is turning out to be ineffectual. In fact, as Albright's star has waned, Kissinger's has risen.

Two years ago, still optimistic about Secretary of State Albright, one journalist wrote in *The Economist,* "Unlike Henry Kissinger (a refugee whose thinking owes more to the Napoleonic wars than to the 20th century), Mrs. Albright has a geopolitical view still shaped by that searing time" of the West's appeasement of Hitler at Munich. Nonsense. If there is any diplomat whose ideas were shaped early, immutably, and meticulously by the experience of Nazism and Munich, it is Kissinger. The problem is that many intellectuals are uncomfortable with what Kissinger seems to have learned as a Jewish teenager in Hitler's Germany. For a long time they believed that he learned little.

Kissinger's first book, *A World Restored: Metternich, Castlereagh and the Problems of Peace 1812–1822* (1957), covers not the Nazi era but the latter part of the Napoleonic Wars and the efforts of European statesmen to build a durable peace afterward. The book's principal character, the Austrian diplomat Prince Clemens von Metternich—secretive, manipulative, and tragic in his worldview—is often seen as the figure Kissinger took as a model, though Kissinger has denied it. Nevertheless, Munich and the Holocaust are ever-present in *A World Restored.* Kissinger, who fled Nazi Germany in 1938, was in the early 1950s trying to claw his way into the stuffy, Protestant-dominated sanctums of the East Coast foreign-policy establishment. He was not about to wear his trauma and his Jewishness on his sleeve, as it is fashionable to do now. Rather, he elegantly camouflaged them. In *A World Restored,* Napoleon plays the Hitlerite role, and Kissinger's answer to the problem of mass evil is contrary to the instincts of liberal humanists. His argument is thus subtle, original, and, I believe, brave.

KISSINGER FIRST ACHIEVED fame as a political scientist with the publication of *Nuclear Weapons and Foreign Policy* (1957), in which he opposed Secretary of State John Foster Dulles's policy of massive nuclear retaliation against a Soviet attack, arguing instead for a flexible response of conventional forces and smaller, tactical nuclear weapons. *A World Restored*—Kissinger's doctoral thesis, which he completed in 1954—is evidence of how the Holocaust, along with the larger record of modern European history, made Kissinger a "realist." The meaning of the term is less clear than it seems.

The very subject of Kissinger's doctoral thesis raised eyebrows at Harvard, as one biographer, Walter Isaacson, has observed. At a time when the threat of thermonuclear extinction obsessed political scientists, the court diplomacy of early-nineteenth-century Europe seemed quaint and irrelevant. Even if the technology of war had changed, Kissinger implied, the task of statesmen remained the same: to construct a balance of fear among great powers as part of the maintenance of an orderly international system—a system that, while not necessarily just or fair, was accepted by the principal players as legitimate. As long as the system was maintained, no one would challenge it through revolution—the way Hitler in the 1930s, categorized by the thirty-year-old Kissinger as a "revolutionary chieftain," did.

It seemed to Kissinger that a world threatened by nuclear disaster could learn much from Metternich. With the British Foreign Secretary Viscount Robert Stewart Castlereagh, Metternich built an order so ingenious that from 1815, the year of Napoleon's defeat at Waterloo, to the outbreak of the First World War, a hundred years later, Europe knew no major conflicts, with the exception of the ten-month-long Franco-Prussian War, in 1870–71. Thanks in significant measure to Metternich, who did everything in his power to forestall the advent of democracy and freedom in the Hapsburg and Ottoman Empires, Europe in 1914 saw peace and steady economic growth as natural and permanent conditions. Europe had thus lost that vital, tragic sensibility without which disaster is hard to avoid, and troops rushed onto the battlefields of Flanders in a fit of romanticism.

When Kissinger wrote, nuclear weapons had altered statesmanship less than we thought—just as new threats such as disease, terrorism, and the breakdown of unstable governments change world politics less than we think. The challenge for diplomats will always be how to maintain a semblance of order through a balance of fear, cooperation, and defensive mechanisms, whether diplomatic, military, or, as in the case of disease, scientific. In an age when borders are weakening and a messier, more cosmopolitan (that is, medieval) world is re-emerging, the story of how Metternich, born in the Rhineland

and more comfortable in French than in German, sought security for a still-feudal Austrian-administered polyglot empire through alliances based on philosophical values rather than ethnic identification is a relevant medicinal.

IN THE FIRST PAGES of *A World Restored,* Kissinger confronted abstractly the 1938 debacle at Munich, in which the British Prime Minister Neville Chamberlain, a progressive reformer who sought peace in order to concentrate on Britain's domestic problems, allowed Hitler to occupy the Bohemian borderlands of Czechoslovakia.

> Those ages which in retrospect seem most peaceful were least in search of peace. . . . Whenever peace—conceived as the avoidance of war—has been the primary objective of a power or a group of powers, the international system has been at the mercy of the most ruthless member of the international community.

Kissinger declared, "It is a mistake to assume that diplomacy can always settle international disputes if there is 'good faith' and 'willingness to come to an agreement' "; in a revolutionary situation "each power will seem to its opponent to lack precisely these qualities." In such circumstances many will see the early demands of a revolutionary power as "merely tactical" and will delude themselves that the revolutionary power would actually accept the status quo with a few modifications. Meanwhile, "Those who warn against the danger in time are considered alarmists."

" 'Appeasement,' " Kissinger concluded, "is the result of an inability to come to grips with a policy of unlimited objectives." A few pages later, for good measure, he added,

> Coalitions against revolutions have usually come about only at the end of a long series of betrayals . . . for the powers which represent legitimacy . . . cannot "know" that their antagonist is not amenable to "reason" until he has demonstrated [that he is not]. . . . And he will not have demonstrated it until the international system is already overturned.

That, of course, is a pitch-perfect description of the late 1930s in Europe. Thus begins a book about how Metternich confronted and undermined the unlimited objectives of Napoleon. In 354 pages there are only three exceedingly brief passing references to Hitler, even as the diplomatic challenge he presented is comprehensively explored.

Kissinger has always been influenced by Munich, if not always directly or humanely. His and President Richard Nixon's opening to China in order to undermine the Soviet Union while they sought détente with Moscow; their unwillingness to quit Vietnam without first wreaking havoc and spilling blood; their support of odious yet pro-American regimes in Greece and Chile; and their brilliantly executed face-off with Syria and the Soviet Union in 1970, at the time of the terrorist challenge to Jordan's pro-Western regime—all flowed to a significant extent from Kissinger's determination to avoid the slightest show of weakness, for which read "appeasement." Kissinger regularly mixed violence and the threat of it with diplomacy, so that the diplomacy had credibility. He preserved what he saw as the legitimate order, in which the Soviet Union was both contained and accepted, so that revolutionary chaos was confined to the edges of the superpower battlefield, in the Third World. (In perceiving the Soviet Union as permanent, orderly, and legitimate, Kissinger shared a failure of analysis with the rest of the foreign-policy elite—notably excepting the scholar and former head of the State Department's policy-planning staff George Kennan, the Harvard historian Richard Pipes, the British scholar and journalist Bernard Levin, and the Eureka College graduate Ronald Reagan.) When, in 1990, Iraq invaded Kuwait, Kissinger argued for military force against Saddam Hussein. The legitimate order in the Gulf had been disrupted by a revolutionary chieftain; to react merely with sanctions would constitute appeasement, and Kissinger said as much.

Kissinger's response to Munich and Nazism in *A World Restored* is pellucid. The key word is "revolution," something that Kissinger's experience as a youth, augmented by scholarship, taught him to fear. Rapid social and political transformation leads to violence, whether throughout the Europe of the early 1800s, owing to Napoleon's aggression—itself a direct result of the French Revolution—or in the Germany of the 1930s. Although the word "revolution" is applied to the America of the 1770s and sometimes to the Zionist movement, the cultural and philosophical awakenings among English settlers in America and Jewish settlers in Palestine took place over decades and were, in truth, evolutions. Iran did experience a revolution in the late 1970s, as did Cambodia in 1975, China in the late 1940s, and Russia in 1917. From his dread of revolutions Kissinger extracted the following principles, which I summarize:

- Disorder is worse than injustice. Injustice merely means the world is imperfect, but disorder implies that there is no justice for anyone, since it makes even the mundane details of daily existence (walking to school, for instance) risky. Obviously, great injustice is worse than a little disorder. In the 1980s Iraq was orderly, so much so that it was like a vast prison, while Iran was in revolutionary chaos. Yet I always felt safer in Iran than in Iraq. I suspect that in Kissinger's fear of disorder there is something deeply personal. In the 1930s he saw Nazism, often in the form of thuggery, overwhelm his seemingly secure physical surroundings. The Nazi thugs he observed were the riffraff cast up first by the civil violence resulting from Germany's defeat in the First World War, and then by the Depression. Kissinger's experience was thus different from that of the humanist Elie Wiesel. Wiesel, who grew up in a secluded Hasidic community in Romania in the 1930s and is five years younger than Kissinger, experienced the Holocaust itself: he spent 1944 and 1945 in Auschwitz and Buchenwald. By then Kissinger was already in the U.S. Army.

- The "most fundamental problem of politics . . . is not the control of wickedness but the limitation of righteousness." The Nazis, the Jacobins, the ayatollahs, and the others who have made revolutions have all been self-righteous. Kissinger suggested that nothing is more dangerous than people convinced of their moral superiority, since they deny their political opponents that very attribute. Tyranny, a form of disorder posing as order, is the result. This was one of Edward Gibbon's arguments against early Christianity. Gibbon represented the Enlightenment in full flower, just as Metternich, Kissinger reminded us, represented its dying breath before the onset of modernism, with its righteous causes. In any event, Kissinger observed wryly, punishing the wicked is "a relatively easy matter, because it is a simple expression" of public decency, and thus not a crucial task of statesmanship.

- Because the real task of statesmen is to forestall revolutions, the real heroes of history are enlightened conservatives such as Metternich and the eighteenth-century Briton Edmund Burke, who fought discrimination against Catholics and opposed the French Revolution for its immoderation. Burke hated revolutions, Kissinger explained, because they violate the average person's sense of morality and well-being; Metternich saw them as contrary to reason. "The true conservative," Kissinger wrote, "is not at home in social struggle. He will attempt to avoid unbridgeable schism, because he knows that a stable social structure thrives not on triumphs but on reconciliations." (The Republican majority in Congress and the "religious right" are thus not true conservatives.) A true conservative is in fact a hesitant progressive: he or she seeks to slow change when society is reforming too fast and to instigate moderate change when society is not reforming at all. Burke's writings are the epitome of this search for pacing. I imagine that Kissinger's tolerance of the late Chinese ruler Deng Xiaoping and his successor, Jiang Zemin, can be explained by the fact that the two Chinese dictators represented enlightened conservatism within their own cultural and historical limits. Both fostered gradual but unmistakable reform that has bettered the material lives of tens of millions of people. At the same time, they averted the kind of revolutionary upheaval that might result from instituting democracy across a vast and geographically riven landscape in which less than 10 percent of the population is middle-class. The Chinese leadership is attempting to treat the dour effects of its decades-old revolution just as Metternich treated Europe after Napoleon's—by doling out moderate doses of change.

The dangers inherent in fast social transformation are so great, Kissinger wrote, that demands for universal justice are ill informed.

> Every statesman must attempt to reconcile what is considered just with what is considered possible. What is considered just depends on the domestic structure of his state; what is possible depends on its resources, geographic position and determination, and on the resources, determination and domestic structure of other states.

THE YOUNG KISSINGER here allied himself with other foreign-policy realists of the time, including Kennan, Reinhold Niebuhr, and Hans Morgenthau. All of them doubted that America, however overarching its power, would ever be able to affect the internal evolution of many other societies at once: the world is too vast, and the expense and stamina required are prohibitive, at least with regard to winning public acceptance. Morgenthau wrote in *Vietnam and the United States* (1965) that because the resources of even a superpower are limited, morality alone can never be a basis for foreign policy. These men saw the missionary idealism of America's ruling elite as naïve. Kissinger believed that idealism had clearly failed throughout America's diplomatic history—that it led to an inefficient cycle of intense hope and activity abroad followed by morose withdrawal once it became apparent that hope and activity were unlikely to remake the world. The clearest example is President Woodrow Wilson's failed attempt to advance democracy and self-determination in the Muslim Middle East after the First World War, and the isolationism that followed.

Kissinger identified the foundations of such idealism when he took up Castlereagh's position on the Greek struggle for independence in 1821, which Metternich opposed. Castlereagh's open-mindedness, Kissinger wrote, reflected not "a superior morality" but rather "the consciousness of safety conferred by an insular position." Because Castlereagh's England was surrounded by seas, it did not have to consider the implications of the breakup of Turkish rule in the Balkans—implications that a Continental power like Metternich's Austria had no choice but to consider. Without America's insular position, guarded by two oceans and reinforced by plentiful natural resources, idealism might never have taken root here. Realism is in part the ability to see the truth behind moral pretensions. Our insular position also explains our failure to see war for what it is: an extension of politics.

I suspect, however, that our much-vaunted foreign-policy idealism is mainly confined to the media and academia, and particularly to the intellectual journals of opinion. Those who sit behind the important desks at the National Security Council, the Departments of Defense and State, and the Pentagon are usually realists. (This is a broad definition, given how often realists disagree: witness Morgenthau's and Kissinger's differing positions over Vietnam.) Even the rare administrations that were associated with foreign-policy idealism converted to realism sooner or later. It was President Jimmy Carter who began what would later be called the "Reagan arms buildup." Traditional Republicans like George Shultz and Caspar Weinberger, and the bipartisan realist Frank Carlucci, became far more influential in the Reagan White House than neoconservative idealists like Elliott Abrams and Jeane Kirkpatrick. For her part, Albright has followed Kissinger's playbook in not overemphasizing human rights in China and in tolerating dictatorships that serve our interests. Realists almost always run foreign policy; idealists, I have found, attend academic conferences and write books and articles from the sidelines.

Take Bosnia. I supported intervention in Bosnia, for strategic and moral reasons. Andrew Kohut, the former president of the Gallup Organization, who is now the director of the Pew Research Center for the People & the Press, told me recently that the polls on Bosnia have, however, been firm and undeniable: at no point in the 1990s, despite all the emotional media coverage and revelations of war crimes, have more than half of the American people thought that U.S. intervention there was warranted. Interventions in Vietnam, Korea, Panama, Grenada, and Iraq were all more popular than our limited and belated one in Bosnia, in late 1995; only the intervention in Haiti, supported mainly by liberal Democrats, was less popular. A former British diplomat, Jonathan Clarke, wrote in his essay "Searching for the Soul of American Foreign Policy" (1995), for the

Woodrow Wilson International Center for Scholars, that Americans "have in fact . . . a rather consistent, well-developed, and finely-calibrated feeling for what does not make sense for their nation's foreign engagements," which in Clarke's view only the illuminati mistake for isolationism. Despite his grave German accent, his dire view of humanity, and his preoccupation with European history, Kissinger—who negotiated with rather than confronted the Soviet Union, who helped Nixon to withdraw from Vietnam 550,000 soldiers in three years under combat conditions, and who generally supported interventions that were popular while expressing skepticism about those that weren't—may have understood his adopted nation better than most people think he did. Indeed, before the March bombing campaign Kissinger implied in an article that forcing Serbia to implement the Kosovo peace agreement might precipitate what the Clinton administration sought to avert: the destabilization of the southern Balkans. Even those of us who believe that the administration had no choice but to use force must admit that Kissinger's analysis was shrewd.

Robert Musil, the Austrian writer, defined realism in *The Man Without Qualities*, his seminal twentieth-century novel, as a political sensibility driven by needs rather than by ideas. Kissinger's description of Metternich's diplomatic achievement in controlling Napoleon adds another layer: "It had not produced any great conceptions; nor had it used the noble dreams of an impatient [revolutionary] generation. Its skill did not lie in creativity but in proportion, in its ability to combine elements it treated as given." Realism is thus about deftly playing the hand that has been dealt you. It is not exciting or inspiring. Journalistic careers are rarely built on embracing realism, though policy-making careers often are.

Metternich, Kissinger wrote, "represented eternal principles not a system." By that Kissinger meant that Metternich was subtle enough to know that systems like autocracy and democracy are indifferent elements; their worth depends on the circumstances under which they operate. Metternich opposed the democratic revolutions in Europe in 1848 not because they were democratic but because they were provoked by ethnic nationalism. Metternich's ultimate achievement was to help postpone (until 1866) the eclipse of a semi-feudal, polyglot Austria by the fiercely modernizing, ethnically nationalist German state to the north. In defending Metternich, Kissinger was at odds with the conventional view of historians, who regard modernism and the independence struggles of 1848 as progressive. Since the end of the Cold War and the unleashing of ethnic nationalism in the former Soviet Union and the Balkans, the Hapsburg monarchy that Metternich served has appeared in a better light.

KISSINGER'S REAL ACHIEVEMENT in *A World Restored* is his writing: a seamless blending of portraiture, philosophy, and international relations. Metternich, Kissinger wrote, was a Rococo figure, complex, finely carved, all surface, like an intricately cut prism. His face was delicate but without depth, his conversation brilliant but without ultimate seriousness. Equally at home in the salon and in the Cabinet . . . he was the *beau-ideal* of the eighteenth-century aristocracy which justified itself not by its truth but by its existence. And if he never came to terms with the new age it was not because he failed to understand its seriousness but because he disdained it. . . . Had Metternich been born fifty years earlier, he would still have been a conservative, but there would have been no need to write pedantic disquisitions about the nature of conservatism. He would have . . . conduct[ed] his diplomacy with the circuitousness which is a symbol of certainty, of a world in which everybody understands intangibles in the same manner. He would still have played at philosophy, for this was the vogue of the eighteenth century, but he would not have considered it a tool of policy. But, in a century of seemingly permanent revolution, philosophy was the only means of rescuing universality from contingent claims.

It is such elegance, thickness of meaning, and narrative ability that puts *A World Restored* into a higher category of literature than the mere policy writings of the rest of the foreign-affairs community. By concentrating on personalities—

Metternich, Castlereagh, Talleyrand—Kissinger demonstrated that policy is not made in an emotional vacuum by "objective" people. The religious and social backgrounds of officials are inseparable from their opinions. Policy making, like lovemaking, is an intensely human activity.

The young Kissinger also realized that a determined policy maker must be in a state of constant tension with the bureaucracy. "Profound policy thrives on perpetual creation. . . . Good administration thrives on routine," he wrote. Foreign Service officers tend to support those policies that do not threaten their jobs and chances for promotion. I have found that many of them just want to get through the day. A Secretary of State who follows these instincts, rather than manipulating and coopting them, is a failed Secretary of State.

This brings me to Kissinger himself, whose personal history caused him to be obsessed with appeasement—sometimes with ironic results. His ideas for maintaining America's share of world power at a time of military debacle abroad and civic disorder at home led him to conduct policy in secret and to battle with the bureaucracy. Like many who seek power in order to do something with it rather than merely to enhance their résumés and self-esteem, he thrived on enemies. Though he has been gone from office for more than two decades, Kissinger hovers over many foreign-policy discussions to a degree that more likable and recent Secretaries of State, such as Shultz and Cyrus Vance, do not.

Both the frequency and the nature of the attacks against

Kissinger avouch his centrality. Criticism of him has often been obsessive and compartmental—and devastating. There are those who despise Kissinger the wiretapper, those who despise him for betraying Cyprus, those who, like me, have faulted him for bombing Cambodia. But when it comes to Kissinger's use of Realpolitik as a counter to America's missionary bent, serious critics have respectfully argued with him more often than denounced him.

A grimly convincing view of the human condition may be all that Kissinger ever had to offer. Despite his historical acumen, he has not always been clairvoyant: for example, he saw the Cold War as continuing indefinitely. Kissinger seems to have lacked the piercing momentary insight that George Ball displayed when he warned the Kennedy and Johnson administrations against further involvement in Vietnam and that Kennan displayed when he suggested that if the West held fast, the Soviet Union would eventually implode. Loy Henderson, a U.S. diplomat, showed that insight time and time again: in the 1930s he was among the first to warn against Stalin; in the late 1940s he was the first to warn against the Soviet threat to the Caucasus and the Aegean; in the early 1950s he was the first to see that the Iranians would one day come to despise us and the first to see through Nehru's idealism and vanity to the anti-Americanism beneath the surface.

Kissinger's perceptiveness has been limited to the present and the past. Although he did not foresee the sudden end of communism, from his study of Castlereagh's dealings with

Czar Alexander I he knew how to approach Moscow: because Russians are so sensitive to unfavorable comparisons with Europeans, try to give them the form if not the substance of what they want. Thus Kissinger wrested Egypt and Syria from the Soviet orbit while inviting Moscow to be a co-host of the late-1973 Middle East peace conference that helped to formalize the new American regional order.

VIETNAM IS THE CRUCIBLE in which Kissinger's realism reached a pitiless extreme, and the one by which he will be judged.

My only approach toward Kissinger himself came in 1991, when I requested an interview with him for a book I was writing about Middle East specialists in the State Department. Kissinger was one of a handful of people, out of the hundreds I asked, who refused to see or even speak to me. Many people I know professionally in the journalistic and policy communities, and whom I respect, despise Kissinger. It is not easy for me to put forward this argument.

Scholars and journalists assert that Nixon and Kissinger might have ended the war in 1969, on terms similar to the ones they settled for in 1973, and prevented the deaths of twenty-two thousand more U.S. combatants; that the two men bombed North Vietnamese cities indiscriminately with B-52s for a negotiating advantage so slight that it was forgotten a few months afterward; and that they waged war in Cambodia illegally and with limited results, except to precipitate the Khmer Rouge takeover in 1975, however unwittingly (a point I made in my book *The Ends of the Earth*).

Kissinger's critics also note that many of these actions were taken not only for policy reasons but also for sometimes sleazy political motives. The secret invasion of Cambodia, William Shawcross asserted in his meticulously researched book *Sideshow: Kissinger, Nixon and the Destruction of Cambodia* (1979), was, among other things, the vehicle Kissinger used to help him consolidate his power within the bureaucracy.

All this I accept. But I believe that other issues should be raised. In the overwhelming majority of foreign-policy crises sordid domestic political motives and interagency infighting play a significant role. So the real questions are What were Kissinger's (and Nixon's) primary rather than secondary motives in continuing the war? and Did their actions have any result beyond the tragic loss of thousands of American and Southeast Asian lives?

Even the harshest journalistic accounts make clear that Kissinger and Nixon genuinely felt, despite the public outcry, that continuing the war was necessary for America to sustain its strategic position worldwide. Shawcross wrote that the two men were influenced by both the "Munich mentality" and the memory of how President Eisenhower ended the Korean War —by threatening the Chinese and the North Koreans. To Kissinger and Nixon, playing tough was not a surrealistic abstraction but something necessary and definable. However wrong the stance they took may appear in hindsight, Kissinger and Nixon did what they thought was right for the country's interests, knowing they would be reviled—especially among the intellectual elite, who usually have the last word in writing history.

Now, isn't that exactly how we want—or at least how we say we want—our leaders to act? Isn't what angers so many people about President Bill Clinton and other current politicians the fact that they make policy according to the results of public-opinion polls rather than to their own conviction? It may be the case that polling is unfairly criticized—that for a leader to base his or her decisions on public opinion is not so bad after all, especially if one has in mind the case of Kissinger and Nixon. It is also likely that in prolonging the war for the reasons they did, Kissinger and Nixon demonstrated more real character than do many of our present leaders.

For the Nixon administration, Vietnam was only one aspect of a larger foreign policy—a policy that brought about significant achievements. To insist that those achievements would have taken place had the administration withdrawn from Vietnam in 1969—and that such an early withdrawal would have gone smoothly—is rash.

To understand the context of those achievements, it is useful to consult the "U.S. History" section of *The World Almanac.* The almanac says that in April 1969 U.S. forces in Vietnam "peaked at 543,400" and "withdrawal started July 8th," six months into Nixon's first term. In 1971 U.S. forces in Vietnam "were down to 140,000" and the "last U.S. combat troops left August 11," 1972. The almanac reports some other facts. During the three years it took the Nixon administration to withdraw combat troops—a year less than it took Charles de Gaulle to end French involvement in the Algerian war, capping his heroic reputation—"Nixon arrived in Beijing Feb. 21 [1972] for an 8-day visit to China. . . . The unprecedented visit ended with a joint communiqué pledging that both powers would work for 'a normalization of relations.' " And "In the first visit of a U.S. president to Moscow, Nixon arrived May 22 for a week of summit talks with Kremlin leaders that culminated in a landmark strategic arms pact." The almanac might also have noted that in September 1970—soon after Nixon made it clear that he was withdrawing slowly, and bloodily, from Vietnam—threats by Nixon to Moscow helped to stop Syrian tanks from crossing farther into Jordan and toppling King Hussein's pro-Western government. One could also note that in 1973 and 1974 Kissinger, serving Nixon and then Gerald Ford, manipulated the Yom Kippur War toward a stalemate that was convenient for American interests, and then brokered agreements between Israel and its Arab adversaries for a separation of forces. These deals allowed Washington to re-establish diplomatic relations with Egypt and Syria for the first time since their rupture following the Six-Day War, in 1967. The agreements also set the context for the Egyptian-Israeli peace treaty of 1979 and helped stabilize relations between Israel and Syria to this day.

The point is not that Nixon and Kissinger withdrew methodically from Vietnam instead of continuing to fight the war that Johnson had escalated by using ground troops, or that elsewhere in the world they performed impressively. Rather, the point is that in the course of conducting the first large-scale American troop withdrawal in our history, under openly humiliating circumstances (more than half a million soldiers of an industrial army were running away from a Third World guerrilla force), the two men actually improved America's geopolitical position vis-à-vis China, the Soviet Union, and the Arab world. This did not occur because of the withdrawal. A typical response I receive when I mention to the political-science community the Nixon administration's withdrawal from Vietnam is "What do you mean, 'withdrawal'? They prolonged the war unnecessarily! And what about the Christmas bombings [against North Vietnam in December 1972] and the attacks on Cambodia [which didn't end until August 1973]?" Indeed, some of Nixon's and Kissinger's actions were so spectacularly brutal, and unnecessary, that they almost obscure the fact of the withdrawal itself. How much more convincing, and nihilistic, can realism get?

Nixon's diplomatic success in China came nearly two months after a heavy air bombardment of North Vietnam, which may have figured in how the Chinese leaders—the hardest of men, whose hands were freshly bloodied by the Great Cultural Revolution—sized up their American visitors. Hans Morgenthau wrote,

The prestige of a nation is its reputation for power. That reputation, the reflection of the reality of power in the mind of the observers, can be as important as the reality of power itself. What others think about us is as important as what we actually are.

In effect, Nixon and Kissinger caused copious bloodshed in Vietnam for the sake of our reputation among our Cold War adversaries: the Chinese and Soviet leaderships and their many clients, including the Syrians. Worse, as Walter Isaacson has written in his biography, Kissinger was suspicious of the whole notion of troop withdrawals that were not tied to improvement in North Vietnamese behavior: that was appeasement. Of course, there is no way to prove or disprove connections between the Nixon administration's cold-bloodedness in Indochina and its ability to project power elsewhere, to America's obvious benefit. Many in the journalistic and policy communities take for granted that there is no connection. Nothing the Nixon administration did in Indochina, therefore, is justified; a Democratic administration would just as easily have faced down the Soviet Union and Syria without firing a shot, and would have orchestrated a rapprochement with China after withdrawing quickly from Vietnam in 1969. Might such reasoning be naïve? Previous behavior is all we have to go on when we respond to others. The suggestion that leaders in China, the Soviet Union, and elsewhere would respond to Kissinger and Nixon based on their recent behavior in Vietnam is eminently reasonable. What strains credulity is the idea that our Cold War adversaries would *not* take into consideration Kissinger's and Nixon's bloodthirstiness in Indochina in the face of fierce criticism from the American public.

In *Decade of Decisions: American Policy Toward the Arab-Israeli Conflict, 1967–1976* (1977), William B. Quandt wrote that Nixon told a group of newspaper editors at the height of the Jordan crisis that "it would not be such a bad thing if the Soviets believed he was capable of irrational action." The strategy worked—it kept the peace in the Middle East that year without U.S. military involvement, and it kept a civilized regime in power in Jordan—perhaps in part because Nixon had already proved his capacity for what many would call "irrational" action. Perceptions are often everything in crises, and Nixon's and Kissinger's record in foreign policy may have been more of a piece than we like to admit.

Was an unproved benefit to our international position worth the loss of so many American and other lives? No. But we will never know for certain what a weaker position in the Middle East and elsewhere might have cost us and others. In 1982, for example, the Israelis invaded Lebanon and bombed Beirut, killing thousands of innocent people. The bombing also drove Yasser Arafat out of Lebanon. From that moment on Arafat's prestige and power plummeted, until a centrist Israeli politician like the late Yitzhak Rabin could afford to recognize him without risking Israel's security. If Arafat were still running his veritable state-within-a-state in Lebanon, the peace process of the 1990s and Jordan's recognition of Israel would be unimaginable. Yet many Israelis, not to mention Arabs, still criticize the late Prime Minister Menachem Begin for bombing Beirut. Was Begin right? It depends.

"TRUTH IS THE successful effort to think impersonally and inhumanly," Musil wrote. Perhaps Kissinger achieved that awful level of truth in Vietnam, to judge by what he and Nixon accomplished coincident with their bloody retreat. If one feels that it is un-American to think of truth in the way that a world-weary Austrian like Musil did, then why does Kissinger's shadowy presence continue to intrude upon our most fundamental foreign-policy questions? Kissinger, seventy-five, can be judged one of our most notable and interesting modern Secretaries of State, along with Dean Acheson, George Marshall, and Henry Stimson—realists all. Americans champion idealism while employing realists, perhaps because we need to have a high opinion of ourselves while pursuing our own interests. Kissinger challenged us with a degree of realism whose origins lay partly in a youthful experience that most Americans can barely imagine.

To say that he has challenged us, of course, is not to say that he has improved us. The final judgment on both Kissinger and Nixon may be that they were not sufficiently realistic. True, they were not swayed by opinion polls, as present politicians so often are. But they did not comprehend that even if the public mood should not dictate policy, policy must nevertheless take account of it. By continuing the war after 1969, they badly misjudged the public's appetite for the conflict. Kissinger thus did not live up to the realism of his literary deal, Metternich. The result of this brand of realism was a foreign policy that some critics call Roman in its cruelty—and in the nonrealist supposition that every corner of the known world is of vital interest to the United States and must be violently defended if necessary. The fact that we have moved away from that policy shows how different our destiny might be from that of Rome's fallen empire.

As regards Musil's inhuman truth, Kissinger's description in *A World Restored* of the peace that followed the Napoleonic Wars bears repeating, for what we may have to expect in the post–Cold War era.

> When peace finally came to Europe . . . it was greeted not only with relief but with a feeling of disillusion as well. The suffering of a period of revolutionary war can be sustained only by millennial hopes, by the vision of a world free of problems. . . . Yet the greater these expectations, the more severe the inevitable disenchantment. There must come a point when it is realized that the exaltation of war is not transferable to the problems of peace, that harmony is an attribute of [wartime] coalitions but not of "legitimate" orders, that stability is not equivalent to the *consciousness* of universal reconciliation. . . . "Everything that occurred after 1815 [follow-

ing the defeat of Napoleon]," Metternich wrote in 1819, "belongs to the course of ordinary history. Since 1815, our period is left to its own devices; it advances because it cannot stop, but it is no longer guided."

We are back to "ordinary history," with the difference between Metternich's and our own time being one of scale—demographic, environmental, technological, and military. Peaceful times are also superficial times, in which we concentrate on social imperfections because the political order appears secure, and judge Cabinet members not on how they perform but on how they perform at press conferences. Such times never last. The end of the Cold War merely set the parameters for the next struggle for survival.

As we seek perfection in our officials through an increasingly intense legal scrutiny, and reap an increasingly sallow form of mediocrity instead, there will come times—perhaps dangerous and violent times—when we will be more forgiving toward those who were supremely imperfect in their character yet unafraid to challenge the public mood. The waging of the decades-long Cold War, which rarely seemed heroic at the time (unless one had the useful corrective, as I and others did, of experiencing firsthand the subjugation of Eastern Europe), is already acquiring a valorous cast. The Soviet Union really did run an "evil empire," and during those years it was absolutely essential for us to maintain a reputation for unflinching firmness. The fact that a few leaders would go to cruel extremes might have been anticipated. Because history is by nature tragic, and because awful choices are certainly part of our future, I suspect that Kissinger—and Nixon, too—will ultimately be judged more charitably. As for Albright, she has yet to be tested nearly to the degree that Kissinger was in Vietnam. She has yet to move emotionally beyond Munich toward Kissinger's ability to turn historical debacle into strategy.

VIII.

CONRAD'S *NOSTROMO*
AND THE THIRD WORLD

(Spring 1998)

THE PROBLEM WITH BOURGEOIS SOCIETIES IS A LACK OF imagination. A person raised in a middle- or upper-middle-class suburban environment, a place ruled by rationalism in the service of material progress, has difficulty imagining the psychological state of affairs in a society where there is little or no memory of hard work achieving its just reward, and where life inside a gang or a drafty army barracks constitutes an improvement in material and emotional security. Even to encounter firsthand such a society—whose instincts have yet to be refined by several generations of middle-class existence—is not enough in the way of an education, since the visitor tends to see it as a laboratory for his or her middle-class ideals, and thus immediately begins to find "evidence" for "pragmatic" solutions. For example, the belief among Clinton administration experts that Haiti—which, with the exception of a U.S. Marine occupation from 1915 to 1934, has not known a civil regime since before the French left in 1804—could be made "democratic" by yet another, even less comprehensive occupation demonstrates how our elites *just don't get it.*

The problem is further compounded by the separation of literature from history and of both from political science in this age of academic specialization, creating policy makers ignorant of the very books that explain places like Haiti and Somalia far better than any social science "methodology." While the usefulness of history is accepted and needs no elaboration, the usefulness of literature is less so among the policy elite, even as Marco Diani, a senior researcher at the Centre National de la Recherche Scientifique in Paris, writes that, "The anguish of any society can be found in its literature, often earlier and more clearly revealed than in its social sciences."* That is because the future lies inside the silences, inside the very uncomfortably sensitive issues that people are afraid to discuss at dinner parties for fear of what others might think of them. And yet it is a principle function of social science to accumulate information precisely on what people are not afraid to talk about in front of a researcher's tape recorder (which is also why conventional journalism is often the most deceptive form of reporting on a society).

Literature, alas, may be the only salvation for the policy elite, because in the guise of fiction a writer can more easily tell

---

*See Diani's introduction to Honoré de Balzac, *The Bureaucrats* (Evanston, Ill.: Northwestern University Press, 1993).

the truth. And in literature's vast canon there is no book of which I am aware that both defines and dissects the problems with the world just beyond our own as well as Joseph Conrad's *Nostromo: A Tale of the Seaboard,* a 1904 novel about Westerners and indigenous inhabitants of an imaginary South American country, Costaguana.* *Nostromo* is neither overly descriptive and moodily vague like Conrad's *Heart of Darkness,* nor is its ending entirely unhappy. For a civil society-in-the-making does emerge in Costaguana, but it is midwived by a ruined cynic of a doctor who has given up on humanity, a deeply skeptical journalist, and two bandit gangs, not by the idealist whose actions had helped lead to the country's earlier destruction. Conrad never denies the possibility of progress in any society, but he is ironic enough to know that "The ways of human progress are inscrutable," and that is why "action is consolatory" and "the friend of flattering illusions." Charles Gould, the failed idealist of the novel, who believes absolutely in economic development, "had no ironic eye. He was not amused at the absurdities that prevail in this world."

Nostromo is at once Conrad's best and most difficult work. It is rather long, 465 pages of small paperback print, and to skim it for even a few paragraphs is to risk losing the thread of the narrative. In this media-obsessed age—when "intellectuals" spend their evenings watching C-SPAN and CNN—people

---

*The version of the novel used here is Joseph Conrad, *Nostromo: A Tale of the Seabord* (New York and Middlesex, Eng.: Penguin Classics, first published 1904).

may be better acquainted with *Heart of Darkness* than with *Nostromo* only because the former is exceedingly short, as well as amenable to skimming, on account of a thin plot and lengthy landscape descriptions. In *Nostromo*, however, landscape ambience is a tightly controlled, strategic accompaniment to political realism. The book is Conrad's "statement on what he thought of as the truth about the world," writes Martin Seymour-Smith in his introduction to the Penguin Classics edition.

It is a tribute to Conrad's insight that his description of Costaguana and its port, Sulaco, captures so many of the crucial tidbits and subtleties about troubled Third World states (particularly small and isolated ones) that foreign correspondents of today experience but do not always inform their readers about, because such details do not fit within the confines of "news" or "objective" analysis. There are, for example, the handful of foreign merchants in Sulaco, without whom there would be no local economy; the small, sovereign parcels of foreign territory (company headquarters and embassies) to which people flee at times of unrest; and the obscure army captain who has spent time abroad hanging about cafés in European capitals, and who later finds himself back home, nursing resentments, and at the head of a rebellion provoked by soldiers who drink heavily. There is, too, the "stupendous magnificence" of the local scenery—what Conrad calls a "Paradise of snakes"; the conspiracy theories begot by deep isolation and the general feeling of powerlessness and "futility"; and a wealthier, more developed part of the country that wants to secede because its inhabitants are even more cynical about the political future over "the mountains" than any foreigner. Conrad shows us, too, how bad forms of urbanization deform cultures: "the town children of the Sulaco Campo," for instance, "sullen, thievish, vindictive, and bloodthirsty, whatever great qualities their brothers of the plain might have had." He describes oscillations between chaos and tyranny, and political movements named after their leaders—Monterists and Ribierists—because in Costaguana, despite the talk of "democracy" and "liberation," there are no ideas, only personalities. He describes "the dread of officialdom with its nightmarish parody of administration without law, without security." He describes a port, an ocean port no less, that because of Costaguana's lawlessness is "so isolated" from the world. His conclusion is of a sort that a novelist can make with less damage to his reputation than a journalist: "The fundamental causes [of the Monterist terror] were the same as ever, rooted in the political immaturity of the people, in the indolence of the upper classes and the mental darkness of the lower." Giorgio Viola, an Italian who fought with Giuseppe Garibaldi and now lives in Costaguana with his dying wife and two daughters, believes, moments after several bullets strike his house and a mob tries to set fire to his roof, that "these were not a people striving for justice, but thieves."

Conrad is relentless in his willingness to confront every unpleasant truth. He will not even admire a beautiful edifice: "The heavy stonework of bridges and churches left by the conquerors," he writes, "proclaimed the disregard of human

labour, the tribute-labour of vanished nations." It is in the total-
ity of his realism that the author—a Pole who knew Russian
tyranny as a boy and later spent fifteen tough years in the mer-
chant marine—achieves fairness. (In one sentence he demol-
ishes North and South: "There is always something childish in
the rapacity of the passionate, clear-minded, Southern races,
wanting in the misty idealism of the Northerners, who at the
slightest encouragement dream of nothing less than the conquest of the earth.") And it is in his sympathy for individuals,
rather than for groups, that Conrad achieves humanity. For
Nostromo, like any great story, is about individuals and their
desperate need for love.

THE FOCUS OF the novel is the defunct San Tome silver mine,
once run by the late father of Charles Gould, an Englishman.
Gould's father had been ruined by corrupt Costaguanan governments that sunk their teeth into his mining profits. Though
his father warned him to stay away from Costaguana and the
mine, Charles Gould returns to restart its operations, confident
that the mine, in addition to making his own fortune, will give
Costaguana the wherewithal to modernize. For like so many
colonialists and idealists (the two are more closely connected
than many think), Gould, Conrad observes,

> cannot act or exist without idealizing every simple feel-
> ing, desire, or achievement. He could not believe his
> own motives if he did not make them first a part of

some fairy tale. The earth is not quite good enough for him.

Gould thinks like many members of the international-aid community: quantitatively, as though determined to avoid any subjectivity whatsoever—even as subjective thinking would have given him to understand what had ruined his father. Gould sees the problems of restarting the mine as merely technical. But it is only when he surmounts the technical difficulties of extracting the silver for handsome profit that the problems to which his father alluded begin. The very success of the mine, rather than creating money for modernization, destabilizes local politics. That is because the mine, and the cash it produces, become—in the absence of other development—a target of malicious rumors and the magnet for local bandit groups to fight over. The mine represents Gould's ingenuity, not that of the indigenous inhabitants; just as oil and natural gas and mineral concerns in the developing world represent the ingenuity of Western corporations that, and that alone, have the organizational and technical know-how to make it all happen. Thus, the fighting that ensues in Costaguana because of Gould's success with the mine is not unlike the violence that wracked Congo-Brazzaville recently, where oil concessions became a treasure over which murderous factions could fight. In such places, Conrad suggests, anything "merely rational fails."

Dr. Monygham, an expatriate English doctor in Costaguana, understands all of this and is determined to help Gould —not because he likes Gould, but because he admires Gould's wife, Emily, who, he realizes, intuits the reality of the country to which her husband appears deaf and dumb. Dr. Monygham is the dark cynic of *Nostromo,* whose very morality is thought to be in question. Dr. Monygham has met "the impossible face to face," through the eyes of dying patients whom he cannot save. He sees through the seductive lie that all situations are clean slates open to broad possibilities. He is wise because he has had experience: the experience of undergoing torture under a previous Costaguanan regime. Torture, Conrad explains, was like a "naturalization" procedure, since it allowed Dr. Monygham to understand life like a true Costaguanan. Indeed, he has become the psychological "slave of a ghost": the ghost of the inquisitorial priest who abused him. (The author alludes to a bright future for torture in the twenty-first century, because as man's passions grow more complex, helped by technological development, his ability to inflict pain on his fellow man will grow infinitely more refined—just look at the twentieth century! Torture may be but an offshoot of progress.) Though Dr. Monygham himself might be beyond redemption, as another character in the story concludes, "He saved us all from the deadly incubus of [the warlord] Sotillo, where a more particular man might have failed."

Another savior of Sulaco—who draws up a blueprint for what would become its successful and humane secession from Costaguana—is Don Martin Decoud, a somewhat radical journalist and among the more intriguing characters in literature. Decoud is a *boulevardier,* a person without accountability, who affects deep concern for humanity and progressive politics in a manner that is at once fashionable and irresponsible. But when he returns from abroad to his homeland, Costaguana, and falls in love with a woman while the country is disintegrating, he is confronted for the first time by a political event that actually matters to his own life. Decoud soon finds himself in a situation whereby he can either help save Sulaco from the warlord Montero, or stand by while the Monterists, once in power, torture him to death. Faced with that, Decoud becomes both devious and heroic, and thus finds his moral salvation through action that, because it is not "merely rational," helps, in an ironic way, to save a whole population from ruin.

Assisting Decoud and Dr. Monygham—I am gravely simplifying a complex plot—are two bandit groups that are no better than the ones that would reduce Sulaco to thuggery. But one of the lessons of *Nostromo* is that in such situations one has to mix with evil in order to deflect it. Among the novel's best moments is when Decoud patiently explains to Mrs. Gould why, in order to save her beloved schools and hospitals, it will be necessary to join forces with the country's most terrifying gang, led by one Hernandez—"the living, breathing example of cruelty, injustice, stupidity, and oppression." Decoud's plan—a savvy one, it turns out—is to make Hernandez a general in the army that will rescue Sulaco.

But the person most crucial to the effort to save Sulaco is the Italian-born leader of the dock workers, Gian' Battista Fidanza, known to the European community as Nostromo, an Italian corruption for "our man." Nostromo is that "fellow in a thousand" who, as a brave, charismatic, and streetwise leader of men (whose personality bridges that of the Europeans and the natives), is the only one who can actually put Decoud's and Dr. Monygham's plan into action. Without Nostromo, the kind of hands-on chap who knows how to safeguard Gould's silver, how to contact the bandit-allies, and much more, the besieged Europeans, for all of their heated discussions and knowledge, would simply be lost.

Here Conrad shows mastery of a situation that Westerners have faced in the Third World through today, especially when such Westerners have the best interests of the indigenous population at heart. I remember that in Khartoum and in Mogadishu during the Horn of Africa famines of the 1980s, and in West Africa during the various crises of the 1990s, the Western-aid community was at the mercy of a handful of local Greeks in Khartoum, of local Italians in Mogadishu, and of local Lebanese in West Africa, all of whom *knew how to do things:* how to obtain visas from the police, how to get cargo through the ports, how to ship food past road blocks—details without which the aid efforts would have collapsed. These people were often cynics: they would smuggle contraband as well as famine relief supplies. But they were cynical because they had experience, and because they had experience they were able to be effective toward a good cause. In the person of Nostromo, Conrad has condensed them all.

Conrad's ending, which I will not give away, is often criticized for its weakness, as if Conrad got tired and did not know how to complete such a great novel. Great books, of course, are not necessarily perfect. But it is possible that the critics are wrong. The last fifty or so pages of *Nostromo* focus on the personal lives and motivations of Dr. Monygham, Decoud, and Nostromo, and particularly on Nostromo's ill-fated love for Giorgio Viola's youngest daughter, Giselle. The novel, in fact, becomes ordinary as the extraordinary political events fade. But isn't this the way life is? Moreover, by nailing down how the most personal of motives were responsible for the political action of these three characters, Conrad places his pessimism where it belongs: within the rubric of humanism. The author shows that even authentic heroes like Nostromo are motivated by personal vanity rather than by ideals, and that such vanity, rather than something bad, is the true source of incorruptibility. Dr. Monygham and Decoud are brave because each wants to impress a particular woman. Nostromo is brave because he seeks a high reputation that is exchangeable for money. Again, I am crudely simplifying complex literary personalities, but the point is that we often do the most noble things in politics for the most personal of reasons, and not for those we publicly espouse. And that is our salvation: because people who are truly "committed" are often the most dangerous, or at least the most sanctimonious. The desire for wealth, or for the admiration of a beautiful woman, may, in fact, preserve objectivity far better than the desire to save a million people.

But how does one convey such truths to the policy community? Even to discuss them is difficult. And it is especially difficult to teach them in the classroom, because so many students who gravitate to political science and journalism these days tend to come from well-off backgrounds and hold idealistic views—as opposed to other young people I have encountered at universities and in the corporate world, from harsher backgrounds, who are unashamed about just wanting "to make money." It is ironically the latter—those with no interest in political science but who have been conditioned as realists—who may be better equipped psychologically to comprehend the situation in many troubled places in the world. Thus, fine fiction like Conrad's may be the only hope for the next generation of journalists and policy makers.

IX.

THE DANGERS OF PEACE

THE ITALIAN POLITICAL THEORIST GAETANO MOSCA noted in *The Ruling Class* (1939) that universal peace is something to be feared, because it could come about "only if all the civilized world were to belong to a single social type, to a single religion, and if there were to be an end to disagreements as to the ways in which social betterment can be attained. . . . Even granting that such a world could be realized, it does not seem to us a desirable sort of world." Of course, there is often nothing worse than war and violent death. But a truism that bears repeating is that peace, as a primary goal, is dangerous because it implies that you will sacrifice any principle for the sake of it. A long period of peace in an advanced technological society like ours could lead to great evils, and the ideal of a world permanently at peace and governed benignly by a world organization is not an optimistic view of the future but a dark one.

Until World War I, war was a respectable endeavor, even a noble one, for war as well as peace often meant progress. What would humanity have become without rebellions! World War I delegitimized war. Its horror was too vast to be justified by any result, especially one so meager. Because a closed elite of generals and diplomats had led humanity into such depths, the result was the popularization of international studies: the birth of modern political science.

Equating early political science with utopianism, the late English historian E. H. Carr in *The Twenty Years' Crisis, 1919–1939* (1939), explains how utopianism was akin to alchemy. When the supply of gold became inadequate for the economic conditions of the fourteenth and fifteenth centuries, alchemists assumed that there must be a way to make it from traditional metals—a problem had arisen for which there must be a solution. In the same way, early political scientists assumed that because war had become so horrible, it must be possible to prevent it: perhaps to outlaw it. But just as you couldn't produce gold from lead, you couldn't declare the end of war either. If you tried, the world was immediately at the mercy of those who disagreed, such as the Nazis and the Japanese military. The appeasement of Hitler had at its roots the absurd notion, propagated by early political science, that war was preventable without results that were even worse. Idealism had gone so far astray that it required an Edwardian-era reactionary who truly respected war, Winston Churchill, to rescue civilization from the brink.

When the North Atlantic Treaty Organization (NATO) was formed in the wake of World War II and U.S. troops were dispatched to Europe, we entered a new condition that offered the attributes of war with the conditions of peace. With violence confined to the Third World, the Cold War left America largely untouched (Korea and Vietnam excepted), even as the conflict with the Soviet Union provided a disciplinary framework so that policy debates, and media coverage of them, were usually serious. Unlike the Augustan Peace that lasted from 31 B.C. to A.D. 14, in which Rome merely stood for order against chaos, the peace of the Cold War allowed the West to define the philosophical terms of its freedom and prosperity by virtue of whom we were up against: for definitions are impossible without boundaries, which often take the form of enemies. Thus, the Cold War may have been as close to utopia as we are ever likely to get. Because the Cold War was a low-level extension of World War II, it also gave us a sense of the past; war does that, peace does not. Recall that the dynamic changes that America went through in the 1950s and 1960s, including the civil rights movement and the erosion of anti-Semitism, would have been impossible without World War II. War, much more than peace, is an equalizer and a fomenter of social change.

But the end of the Cold War did not return us to the conditions of peace that we knew at the end of our previous wars, since the effect of technology on weaponry and geography had made the world both more volatile and closer than ever. And because the Cold War went on for so long, it created a military es-

tablishment too vast and knowledgeable about the details of crisis management for it to retreat to the periphery. Yet, even as
the military is now engaged in foreign policy to an unprecedented degree, with the chairman of the Joint Chiefs of Staff,
General Henry H. Shelton, a virtual member of the inner cabinet and the commander in chief of Central Command, General
Anthony C. Zinni, a virtual proconsul for the Middle East, the
society at large (as I will illustrate) has fallen under the numb-
ing and corrosive illusion of peace.

AVOIDING TRAGEDY REQUIRES a sense of it, which in turn requires a sense of history. Peace, however, leads to a preoccupation with *presentness,* the loss of the past and a consequent
disregard of the future. That is because peace by nature is plea-
surable, and pleasure is about momentary satisfaction. In an
era of extended domestic peace, those who deliver up pleasures
are the power brokers. Because pleasure is inseparable from
convenience, convenience becomes the vital element in society.

"The mass man loves gags," writes Saul Bellow in his introduction to the Spanish philosopher José Ortega y Gasset's 1929
work *The Revolt of the Masses.* "He is a spoilt child, demanding
amusement, given to tantrums. . . . His only commandment is
Thou shalt expect convenience." Ortega y Gasset's "mass man"
is the self-satisfied specialist in a postindustrial society who
knows expertly his own corner of the universe but is ignorant of
the rest: a "learned ignoramus." The mass man, writes Ortega y

Gasset, "is obviously interested in automobiles, anesthetics, and all manner of sundries. And these things confirm his profound lack of interest in civilization itself. For all these things are merely products of civilization, and the passion he displays for them makes more crudely obvious his insensibility to the principles which made them possible." Ortega y Gasset also says that a "world overabundant in possibilities" for the mass man "automatically produces grave deformities, vicious forms of human existence. . . ." Dictated by convenience and gratification, the mass man realizes no limits to his pleasures. And "barbarism," Ortega y Gasset reminds us, "is the absence of norms and of any possible appeal based on them."

If Ortega y Gasset overstates his case, that is because we have not yet had enough years and decades of domestic peace for the mass man to truly come into his own. Reflect on how American society has progressed (or deteriorated) since the end of the Cold War, and then project ahead several decades, while including the exponential cultural effect of rapid technological innovation, and one may glimpse the conundrum of America at peace.

In an era when peace is taken for granted, the electronic media increasingly adopt the aspirations of the mob. The mob, like the television camera, has no historical memory and is entirely reductive: it considers only what is within its field of vision, not the complicating facts beyond it. What did the American anchors at Princess Diana's funeral represent except the emotions of the mob, consolidated into a few insipid

voices? Peace enlarges the scope and intensity of such phenomenon, because with nothing of truly life-and-death importance
at stake, the media require less accountability. And because
the media increasingly lack both irony and a sense of the past,
they concentrate on public scandal, unaware that a system with
little or no corruption would likely be tyrannical: Hitler's Germany, Mengistu Haile Mariam's Ethiopia, and Lee Kuan Yew's
Singapore represent, among other things, relative honesty in
bureaucracy. Corruption, infidelity, and stupidity in moderate
doses are, like occasional wars, evidence of humanity.

In an extended era of domestic peace, government institutions appear less vital because national security is assumed,
and the memory of it being directly challenged has faded. Less
sacrosanct than ever, government institutions become easier to
attack, especially as, with thousands of employees making tens
of thousands of daily decisions, corruption at some level must
always occur in a nontyrannical regime. Too many ambitious,
outside experts and too much information must eventually undermine institutions, since bureaucracies—composed as they
are by ordinary people who aren't well paid—require a reasonable berth of error merely to function. Because information as
it is disseminated to a large and imperfectly educated audience
becomes vulgarized, the media—and well-heeled pressure
groups with access to it—will increasingly create mass hysteria
over single issues by the crude dispersion of facts untempered
by context. Whereas war leads to a respect for large, progressive
government, peace creates an institutional void filled by,

among other things, entertainment-oriented corporations. True peace would show just how serious the questions of the existentialists really are. Contrary to what some may think, existentialism is more than a European intellectual affectation. It addresses the search for meaning in existence at a time when no such search appears necessary, because existence has never been threatened in anyone's living memory.

A more concretely frightening prospect of peacetime is the reduction of standing armies. Mosca notes in *The Ruling Class* that because every society throughout history contains a crucial percentage of males driven to impulsive physical action, one purpose of standing armies has been to canalize and bureaucratically control this violent element of the citizenry, and steer it toward a useful end. Therefore, a reduced standing army will likely result in an increase in gang activity and other forms of violent behavior. For example, militias were far less popular during the age of conscription because when everybody had to serve, khaki uniforms and what they suggested carried no mystique. With our standing army set to diminish further and to gradually transform itself into a more elite, corporate-style force—in which knowledge of foreign languages and other forms of academic achievement will be increasingly valued—there are likely to be more frustrated, action-prone, young males in America with no acceptable outlet for their inclinations. So the idea that a world at peace will mean less violence is naïve. We will have as much violence as before, only it won't take an organized form, and will lack redeeming philosophical value. Of course, we can lower our crime rates (as we have) by making potential victims less vulnerable—through more prisons, electronic surveillance, and gated communities. One can see the pattern, though: true peace, of the kind many imagine, is obtainable only through a form of tyranny, however subtle and mild.

WHEN PEOPLE IMAGINE a world at peace they often imagine it within the framework of a strong United Nations. Though a more powerful U.N. would serve everyone's interests in the broad field of humanitarian assistance, a really politically muscular international organization is undesirable.

A U.N.-governed world is interesting to contemplate in the abstract because it fits the scenario of peace feared by Mosca: a world in which there are no fundamental disagreements about the ways of social betterment; for if there were, the great powers would not have ceded control of many matters to the U.N., which allows us to describe this hypothetical world as "U.N.-governed" in the first place. In such a world, a unified global elite agrees on how to fight disease, poverty, global warming, dictatorship, drug smuggling, trade barriers, and so forth. The problem with this vision is that there are no universal truths on how to organize society or improve it. The cannon of humanism emphasizes that we cannot know everything about ourselves, that we will forever remain a sanctified mystery. It is not that we are doomed to be individuals and, therefore, to disagree: on the contrary, such disagreements are precisely what clarify our *humanness*. Even with such obvious villains as drug smugglers, as we have learned from our diplomatic disputes with Mexico and Colombia, there will be deep divides, based on geography, history, and so on, about how to deal with them.

The U.N. represents not just the hopes but more accurately the illusions of millions of people, from those in Third World villages to university liberal arts departments, who want to escape from the historical cycle of war and power politics, and miss or deny the point that the U.N. is a forum for the same power politics in disguise, with the divisions of the Cold War eventually replaced by others.

Whereas World War I delegitimized war, the end of the Cold War has spawned an equally dangerous notion: the delegitimization of great power divisions. As the late French humanist Raymond Aron wrote in *Peace and War: A Theory of International Relations* (1966), "The idealist, believing he has broken with power politics, exaggerates its crimes." U.N. Secretary-General Kofi A. Annan may be one such idealist. In a January 1999 *New York Times* op-ed piece, he wrote, "A divided [security] council can, and has in the past, paralyzed the United Nations. I must and will do all in my power to avoid such a fate." Annan thus misses the point of the Cold War: that it was actually about something, rather than a value-neutral affair in which both sides were unfortunately divided. Indeed, because the Cold War was a totemic struggle of enlightened values versus despotic ones, divisions such as those in the Security

Council were far more preferable than any compromising unanimity. As a reporter in the communist Balkans, Soviet-occupied Afghanistan, and Marxist Ethiopia in the 1980s, I saw that division in the U.N. was something to be proud of. The U.N. as an institution might have been weakened by it, but not humanity. The "universal values" of the U.N. Charter are those of the victorious Western Allies of World War II—not those of the East Bloc or the "Zionism is Racism" Third World, upon which many U.N. Cold War majorities depended. (Moreover, the enhanced "moral promise" of the U.N. that Annan mentions in his op-ed article was won not by the General Assembly or the U.N. Secretariat in 1989, but by East European dissidents, Pope John II, and NATO Cold Warriors.)

The U.N. bureaucracy, along with others who seek a peaceful world, worship consensus. But consensus can be the handmaiden of evil, since the ability to confront evil means the willingness to act boldly and ruthlessly and without consensus, attributes that executive, national leadership has in far more abundance than any international organization. As Aron writes, "prudence does not always require either moderation or peace by compromise, or negotiations, or indifference to the internal regimes of enemy states," and that is why "war has not always been meaningless or criminal; it has had meaning and function." Thus, there is an inherent philosophical danger in a strong secretary-general who can prevent or postpone war even when war is necessary to fight evil.

And because morality is unachievable without amoral

force, the re-authorization of assassinations by the U.S. Congress might do much more to contain evil than enlarging the Security Council to include nations such as India and Brazil (as some propose), in which case consensuses would be even harder to achieve at the U.N., and would thus be based on a common denominator so low as to be meaningless. Such an enlarged council would always be claiming to do magnificent things for humanity, while rarely doing anything specific.

Rather than a better version of humanity, a world body merely reflects the global elite as it is. Until recently, the U.N. has been, to a significant degree, strongly influenced by a Third World aristocracy, those whose families have acquired wealth and prestige in their own societies through various means, often unmeritocratic, often without having to pay income taxes. To this unmeritocratic elitism, add a northern European element that implicitly trusts bureaucracy—because its own historical experience has been within tight, uniethnic societies where the functionary is "the man next door." The result has been a luxury air lock where formality and ritual are key, and phraseology masks unpleasant on-the-ground truths to an extent greater than in the U.S. Congress, whose redeeming humanity is exemplified by its very buffoonery and lack of sophistication. Though the U.N. is certainly not about to dominate the world, it carries within it the seeds of a banal, bureaucratically distant organization, inflexible because of the vast territory it would have to manage, and lacking accountability because of its received claim to progressive rationality. Such an organization would rule not through violence but by ably de-legitimizing—perhaps, with the help of an all-powerful global media—anything and anybody that crossed its path, by defin-ing such opposition as "immoral," "unprogressive," "provin-cial," or "isolationist."

We think we know what *political correctness* is: we have no idea how intensely suffocating public discourse could become in a truly unified and peaceful world.

The more global, the more aloof and sanctimonious—that would be the core problem with a politically powerful U.N. To wit, the U.N., already dominated by a highly bureaucratized elite that preaches democracy—but in the case of many of its functionaries has no profound experience of it—and has no aim or value system above the avoidance of violent conflict, would in the future be easily dominated by an aristocracy of technical experts: what the nineteenth-century French philoso-pher Auguste Comte called a scientific priesthood.

Thus, the U.N. should remain a tool of shifting coalitions and great power struggles, which, in turn, reflect basic and honest divisions among humanity. Nor do physical threats to the earth like asteroids or climate change necessarily argue for global governance. Because of the technological prowess re-quired, an efficacious response to such challenges could only be mounted by a concert of great powers, who may or may not employ the legitimizing mechanism of the U.N. As for a global constabulary force to intervene in humanitarian tragedies, as Bosnia showed, such a force is more likely to emerge from NATO than from the U.N. That is because military coalitions tend to emerge from a nucleus of powers who, for historical and cultural reasons, tacitly trust each other enough to share intelligence data.

THIS BRINGS ME to the role of the United States: a role necessary not only for minimal global security but for the health of our own society, which is beginning to suffer from the deformities of domestic peace.

Because, as Carr notes in *The Twenty Years' Crisis*, international goals are best realized through national self-interest, the President of the United States should project power through the U.N. to the benefit of both. The U.S. should pay its dues and, in essence, without declaring it, take over the U.N. in order to make it a transparent multiplier of American and Western power. That, of course, may not lead to peace, since others might resent it and fight as a result; but such an action would fill the world organization's insipid ideological vacuum with at least someone's values—indeed, ours. Peace should never be an expediency. Whether it was the Korean War, the 1991 Gulf War, or the weapons-inspection regime against Saddam Hussein, the U.N. has always been most credible when it was an accomplice of U.S. foreign-policy goals.

The American takeover of the U.N. may already be happening—to the degree, that is, that the Republican Congress will allow. Indeed, the Republican Right, while it worries plausibly about the loss of traditional values in an era of peace, is an example of the deformities it decries, since historically prosperous societies which perceive no outside threat have been the only ones that have the luxury to preoccupy themselves with discussions about such things as sexual values. The problem, though, is that we have no such luxury. The peace we think we have is only an interregnum before another cycle of conflict. The narcissistic isolationism of the congressional Republicans—who call for enforcing democracy abroad while denying the State Department the tools it requires for our own security interests and who refuse to pay our U.N. dues—comes at a time when the world vaguely resembles what it was before the outbreak of World War I.

As then, there are legions of techno-optimists celebrating the expansion of world trade and claiming that human ingenuity will solve our problems, neglecting to mention that human ingenuity usually arrives too late to solve the specific problem for which it was intended. Like then, new categories of products are available to an expanding world middle class, even as new sources of oil and other raw materials are discovered. Like then, a conventional wisdom says that the mounting interdependency of financial markets make large-scale conflagration impossible. Like then, beneath the surface of comforting, globalizing truths, the world is awash in dangerous new alliances. For example, despite the myth of a reunited Europe, Europe has redivided along historical-civilizational patterns, with the recently expanded NATO a variation of the Western Holy Roman Empire, and the Eastern Orthodox world of Russia, Romania, Bulgaria, and much of the former Yugoslavia left out, embittered, and economically falling off the map. Like a century ago, there is much new weaponry that now, because of postindustrial miniaturization, is concealable even as it is more deadly: the perfect tools for stateless terrorists of which the world has enough. The clock ticks toward something unpleasant, while our entertainment culture dilates to the point that the Academy Awards ceremony has achieved a status akin to a national holiday.

FOR OTHER REASONS, too, the vision of a world at peace is unrealistic.

A long domestic peace would rear up leaders with no tragic historical memory, and thus little wisdom. Nor would such future leaders be fortified by a life of serious reading to compensate for their lack of historical experience: permanent peace, with its worship of entertainment and convenience, will produce ever-shallower leaders. The mass man will rule as well as be ruled. Nor would such childlike leaders be well advised, due to the inverse relationship between wisdom and specialization. The men and women around these future peacetime leaders would tend to be specialists; that is true not only of the scientific priesthood, but also of those educated in the social sciences. The sheer accumulation of texts produces people conditioned to jargon and arcane monographs, yet increasingly ignorant of great philosophy. Think of the mentality of young White House aides after, say, sixty years of domestic peace, and you may grasp why even if peace obtains for sixty years, it could not for sixty-one.

Such shallow leaders and advisers would, by the very virtue of their lack of wisdom and experience, eventually commit the kind of ghastly miscalculation that would lead to a general war of some kind. The experience following the turn of the twentieth century shows this tragic cycle of historic self-correction at work. After the Napoleonic Wars, many decades of peace in Europe led to rulers who lacked a tragic sense of the past, which caused them to blunder into World War I.

The solution for such trends is simple: struggle, of one sort or another, hopefully nonviolent. Struggle demands the real facts, as well as real standards of behavior. While governments lie in specific instances during wartime, war ultimately demands credibility, whereas long periods of peace do not; with no threat at hand, lies and exaggerations carry smaller penalties. Struggle causes us to reflect, to fortify our faith, and to see beyond our narrow slots of existence. A world of natural limits, in which clean air and water and fecund soil were highly prized commodities, might impose a sense of warlike reality upon us, preventing us from becoming barbarian mass men, yet without requiring the citizenry to fight. What we should be skeptical of are the "benefits" of a world at peace with unlimited natural resources. As Ortega y Gasset reminds us: "nobility is synonymous with a life of effort."

True peace and security, of course, are impossible, and that may be to the good. Robert Lowell, in his poem "For the Union Dead," about the monument on the Boston Common dedicated to the African-American Civil War heroes killed in South Carolina in 1863, upholds "man's lovely, peculiar power to choose life and die," while condemning the "savage servility" of Ortega y Gasset's mass man.* We must seek a compromise between that monument on Boston Commons, honoring humankind's willingness to fight for what it believes in, and the monument outside the U.N. building, recommending that we *beat our swords into plowshares*. For to use only the latter monument as a compass point would be to head into oblivion.

---

*Robert Lowell, *For the Union Dead* (New York: Farrar, Straus & Giroux, 1960).

INDEX

ABOUT THE AUTHOR

ROBERT D. KAPLAN is a correspondent for *The Atlantic Monthly* and the author of six previous books on travel and foreign affairs that have been translated into a dozen languages. His bestseller *Balkan Ghosts* was chosen by *The New York Times Book Review* as one of the best books of 1993 and by Amazon.com as one of the top ten travel books of all time. *An Empire Wilderness, The Ends of the Earth* (also bestsellers), and *The Arabists* were all chosen by *The New York Times* as notable books of the year in 1998, 1996, and 1993, respectively. *An Empire Wilderness* was chosen by *The Washington Post* and the *Los Angeles Times* as one of the best books of the year. He lectures frequently to the U.S. military and was a consultant to the U.S. Army's Special Forces Regiment and is a fellow with the New America Foundation. He has written the Introduction to the Modern Library's edition of Joseph Conrad's *Lord Jim & Nostromo*. He lives with his wife and son in western Massachusetts.

ABOUT THE TYPE

This book was set in Scala, a typeface
designed by Martin Majoor in 1991.
It was originally designed for a music
company in the Netherlands and then
was published by the international type
house FSI FontShop. Its distinctive
extended serifs add to the articulation
of the letterforms to make it a
very readable typeface.